Please May I Have My Football Back?

The record 125 Years of

the Alexander Family at Manchester City

ERIC ALEXANDER

KNOW THE SCORE BOOKS SPORTS PUBLICATIONS

CRICKET	Author	ISBN
ASHES TO DUST	Graham Cookson	978-1-905449-19-4
BEST OF ENEMIES	Kidd & McGuinness	978-1-84818-703-0
BODYLINE HYPOCRISY	Michael Arnold	978-1-84818-702-3
CRASH! BANG! WALLOP!	Martyn Hindley	978-1-905449-88-0
GROVEL!	David Tossell	978-1-905449-43-9
KP: Cricket Genius?	Wayne Veysey	978-1-84818-701-6
MOML: THE ASHES	Pilger & Wightman	1-905449-63-1
MY TURN TO SPIN	Shaun Udal	978-1-905449-42-2
WASTED?	Paul Smith	978-1-905449-45-3

CULT HEROES	Author	ISBN
CARLISLE UNITED	Mark Harrison	978-1-905449-09-7
CELTIC	David Potter	978-1-905449-08-8
CHELSEA	Leo Moynihan	1-905449-00-3
MANCHESTER CITY	David Clayton	978-1-905449-05-7
NEWCASTLE	Dylan Younger	1-905449-03-8
NOTTINGHAM FOREST	David McVay	978-1-905449-06-4
RANGERS	Paul Smith	978-1-905449-07-1
SOUTHAMPTON	Jeremy Wilson	1-905449-01-1
WEST BROM	Simon Wright	1-905449-02-X

MATCH OF MY LIFE	Editor	ISBN
DERBY COUNTY	Nick Johnson	978-1-905449-68-2
ENGLAND WORLD CUP	Massarella & Moynihan	1-905449-52-6
EUROPEAN CUP FINALS	Ben Lyttleton	1-905449-57-7
FA CUP FINALS 1953-1969	David Saffer	978-1-905449-53-8
FULHAM	Michael Heatley	1-905449-51-8
IPSWICH TOWN	Mel Henderson	978-1-84818-001-7
LEEDS	David Saffer	1-905449-54-2
LIVERPOOL	Leo Moynihan	1-905449-50-X
MANCHESTER UNITED	Ivan Ponting	978-1-905449-59-0

STOKE CITY	Simon Lowe	978-1-905449-55-2
SUNDERLAND	Rob Mason	1-905449-60-7
SPURS	Allen & Massarella	978-1-905449-58-3
WOLVES	Simon Lowe	1-905449-56-9

GENERAL FOOTBALL	Author	ISBN
2006 WORLD CUP DIARY	Harry Harris	1-905449-90-9
BEHIND THE BACK PAGE	Christopher Davies	978-1-84818-506-7
BOOK OF FOOTBALL OBITUARIES	Ivan Ponting	978-1-905449-82-2
BURKSEY	Peter Morfoot	1-905449-49-6
FORGIVE US OUR PRESS PASSES	Football Writers' Association	978-1-84818-507-4
JUST ONE OF SEVEN	Denis Smith	978-1-84818-504-3
LEFT BACK IN TIME	Len Ashurst	978-1-84818-512-8
MAN & BABE	Wilf McGuinness	978-1-84818-503-6
MY PREMIERSHIP DIARY	Marcus Hahnemann	978-1-905449-33-0
OUTCASTS	Steve Menary	978-1-905449-31-6
The Lands That FIFA Forgot		
PALLY	Gary Pallister	978-1-84818-500-5
PARISH TO PLANET	Dr Eric Midwinter	978-1-905449-30-9
A History of Football		
TACKLES LIKE A FERRET	Paul Parker	1-905449-47-X
(England Cover)		
TACKLES LIKE A FERRET	Paul Parker	1-905449-46-1
(Manchester United Cover)		
WARK ON	John Wark	978-1-84818-511-1

RUGBY LEAGUE	Author	ISBN
MOML WIGAN WARRIORS	David Kuzio	978-1-905449-66-8
MOML LEEDS RHINOS	Caplan & Saffer	978-1-905449-69-9

Please May I Have My Football Back?

The record 125 Years of
the Alexander Family at Manchester City

ERIC ALEXANDER

www.knowthescorebooks.com

First published in the United Kingdom
by Know The Score Books Ltd, 2008
© copyright Eric Alexander

Know The Score Books Limited
118 Alcester Road
Studley
Warwickshire
B80 7NT
01527 454482
info@knowthescorebooks.com
www.knowthescorebooks.com

A CIP catalogue record is available for this book from the British Library
ISBN: 978-1-84818-508-1

Jacket design by Graham Hales

Printed and bound by Athenaeum Press, Gateshead, Tyne & Wear

Photographs: Manchester Evening News, Stockport Express, Daily Express, Picture Coverage Ltd, the Alexander Family & Clive Cooksey

ACKNOWLEDGEMENTS

Over the years I have cooperated with the Media in all its forms: Radio. Television, Film-making, the Press and authors by giving interviews, opinions and supplying facts and considerable memorabilia. It is due to the encouragement of several remaining friends in these fields, or perhaps their sensing retribution, that I have decided to dip my toe into murky waters by telling stories and experiences from behind the scenes of what, despite our triumph in the Rugby World Cup in 2003, the Ashes in 2005 and the predominance of 'overseas' players and managers, is still called our National Game.

In my experience, books written by players and former managers generally tend to treat directors and club officials with a certain amount of disdain, if not ridicule. So it may make a change for a version of what being an integral part of a major football club is like to come from someone like me who has been involved with Manchester City at board level from pram to president. Football has changed beyond all recognition during my lifetime and in these pages I discuss and reminisce about my personal experiences as a director and senior figure at both Maine Road and all Lancashire football.

And what a journey it has been! Bell, Summerbee, Lee, Corrigan, Marsh, Mercer, Allison, Best, Charlton, Law, Book and Pardoe; Cup and league success, global travel, takeovers, egos, international incidents, underfloor heating, sponsorship, a fond farewell to Maine Road, the arrival of the Sheiks at 'Middle Eastlands', bombs and prostitution. It's all here!

A dislike of books written in the first person singular (or 'as we was taught' at Manchester Grammar School, the personal pronoun 'I') has always given me a problem, but there does not appear a way around it if this assortment of memories and tales is to come across as a personal tale, rather than a droning book, or monologue. Your tolerance and understanding that this is for documentary reasons, rather than conceit, would be appreciated.

For discussing incidents as I went along and confirming facts I wish to thank the following friends: Ken Barnes, Colin Bell, Richard Bott, Ricky Broadbent, John Bullen, Jim Cassells, Daren Clarke, Gary Clarke, Harry Finlaison, Steve Fleet, Peter Gardner, Bernard Halford, Walter Harrison, Johnny Hart, Gary James, Geoff Karran, Francis Lee, Ian Niven, Glyn Pardoe, Ken Parker, Sidney Rose, Brian Warburton, Johnny Williamson, the late Ian Wooldridge and Alec Johnson. Really most of all I would like to say a hearty 'thank you' for the years of friendship, which to me is what life is all about.

This book has been written for the benefit of my children, their children and, hopefully, future generations of the family. I believe it important to know about your ancestors, good, bad or indifferent.

Eric Alexander
October 2008

There are three difficulties in authorship:
To write anything worth publishing;
To find honest men to publish it;
And to get sensible men to read it.

Colton

I have assembled these facts as I have been able to learn
them from ancient documents, listening to old men talk and
my own personal knowledge.

The Venerable Bede, 673-735

As the boy said,
"Hey, Mister. Please may I have my football back?"

CONTENTS

Rather than normal chapters, this book has been divided into two halves, split by a short half-time break, extra time, penalties and an occasional throw-in. The second half is a bit longer than the first, rather like a match on Fergie's watch – surely the most inaccurate timepiece since the Mad Hatter's.

Eventually experts have convinced me that there is an interesting story to be told, certainly unique in the annals of British football and in 'Pre-Season Training' you can appreciate how I came by the title.

First Half:
Background to football firsts, e.g. professional players, changes to rules which have affected the World game and significant landmarks that have emanated from the Lancashire Football Association and consequently my family and our parts played in these developments. My grandfather gave many years service and was a Vice President of the LFA. I have given 30 years service and am a Life Vice President, in addition to serving 25 years on the Executive Council of the Lancashire Football League, the principal professional league in the North for the junior sides of the top League clubs, my father being an instigator of the League and thirty nine years in charge of Manchester City's junior teams. My own playing and development years, which are not self-laudatory but perhaps give an insight into my attitude and build up of experience, which in the opinion of some experts is unique.

Half-time:
Quick review of events leading to my becoming a Director of Manchester City.

Second Half:

My years and experiences, home and abroad, whilst a Director and Chairman of a very successful League club with incidents, humorous and serious, concerning household names and my part in the development of equipment, playing surfaces, sponsorship and stadium design etc., the truth about incidents relating to personalities, takeovers and myths that have been perpetuated by hearsay as opposed to facts. I know because I was there.

Extra-time:

My opinions on football, personalities and the game in the 25 years since I resigned as a Director.

Penalties:

Discussion on the development of the current situation with clubs facing bankruptcy and extinction, foreign money, overseas players, lack of opportunity for our youth, attitudes to authority and possible remedies.

PRE-SEASON TRAINING

Former Manchester City and England goalkeeping legend Frank Swift wrote a book entitled *Football From The Goalmouth*, goalscorer supreme Tommy Lawton called his *Football Is My Business*, Peter Doherty, that delightful artist with the ball for City and Ireland, chose *Spotlight On Football*, and another City goalkeeper, former German POW Bert Trautmann, went for *Steppes To Wembley*. All very interesting and appropriate titles, and I too was faced with the task of finding a name for this collection of reminiscences which would stir a few people into reading it.

I was previously talked – bribed is probably more accurate – into writing a book on golf, for a particular club's Centenary and its effect on the life of a village over the one hundred years. A title evaded me until it was finished, whereupon I settled for a parody of Mark Twain's famous comment and called it *Definitely Not A Good Walk Spoiled*. This appears to have been well received in many quarters, incuding the Royal & Ancient. But what to call this tale, a story of over 125 years in the making, of grandfather, son and grandson continuously involved in the running of professional, and to a lesser degree amateur, football? Originally, *Outside Left To The Chair To Left Outside* appealed to my rather odd sense of humour, but it is not quite accurate as my involvement in soccer still causes me sleepless nights and the inevitable boredom of well-meaning people in pubs telling me how to put the football world to rights. To misquote George Burns:

'Too bad all the people who know how to run football are too busy driving taxis or cutting hair.'

I am well aware that my book has to be unusually interesting and different, as the market place is flooded these days with the life stories of players barely out of nappies, or men of yore trying to supplement their pensions, ghost written by eager scribes lusting after satellite fame and fortune. These epistles generally start off in a blaze of publicity at twenty quid and a month later are on the sale shelves at a fiver and it will count as a minor miracle if this effort even starts off on the cut price shelves or at a car boot sale.

Some twenty years ago when I resigned as a Director of Manchester City to become the Honorary Life President, offers poured in from the media of the day for an exposé on football in general and Manchester City in particular. Tempting though the thought of getting even with one or two s***s may have been, I believed, in fact I knew, that it could have caused great damage to both the Club and professional football in general. But, having passed the three score and ten and with my life entering into extra time, now seems a good time to talk openly about a lifetime spent in professional football.

It would be easy to blow away some popular beliefs, myths, reputations and possibly put a few marriages under pressure if I told the unexpurgated truth, but that is neither my style or intention. These are honest recollections of happy, humorous, serious, exciting and disappointing times and the truth regarding several misconceptions which, hopefully, will be put into perspective. It is also not my intention to write a book just about Manchester City, and although my background makes that the predominant club during my career I have considerable experience of other footballing matters that I hope will create some interest for you. Unfortunately the political correctness of today's World cramps my sense of humour, prevents the repetition of several entertaining tales and has reduced my available material.

It has taken me the best part of four years to put all this together, as and when the mood has taken me, so there are topics, decisions and situations that may have changed since the initial views but I have not necessarily up-dated my opinions because you could go on forever, given the way the game has gone, and continues to go down the slippery path. I have not used a 'Ghost Writer', the words and spellings are my own, I have typed every word with my two middle fingers and the truth should never be libelous.

I hope you persevere and enjoy the book . . . if not, you can always give it to somebody you don't like as a Christmas present.

Comment is free, but facts are sacred.

Eric Alexander
March 2009

FIRST HALF

1933

NOW THERE'S A YEAR FOR YOU . . .

92,000 people at Wembley Stadium saw Everton beat Manchester City 3-0 in the FA Cup final. This was the first occasion numbers were put on the back of players' shirts, Everton wore 1 to 11 and City 22 (goalkeeper Frank Swift) to 12.

The Australians whinged about Douglas Jardine's England's 'bodyline' bowling as our cricketers brought back the Ashes.

Backless dresses (for ladies, that is) became acceptable in polite society.

Franklin Delano Roosevelt became the 42nd President of the United States of America, survived an assassination attempt and abolished prohibition.

Adolf Hitler and his Nazis took over Germany.

Film star Marlene Dietrich caused a sensation by appearing in Paris dressed in men's clothing, starting a fashion craze that is still with us (well, some of us).

On that note, football shorts were still officially called 'knickers'.

All these and other fascinating events somewhat overshadowed the arrival in a quiet south Manchester suburb of one Albert Eric Alexander.

It had been anticipated that I would make my debut on the Isle of Man, where for many years my family and their friends had spent the summers. However such was my mother's apparent haste to part with me that I was born a little early and mucked up the holiday arrangements. After some two weeks my mother had not recovered properly and had fallen ill. Some unkind folk, including a few Manchester United and Liverpool supporters, say I still have that effect on people. She went back into hospital and my very kind Auntie Kitty and Uncle Harry took me into their home at Harrogate in Yorkshire for a few weeks while she was sick. By the time I returned we had moved house to near Styal, close to where Manchester Airport is today, so although being a Mancunian by birth, I have only ever lived in Lancashire for a couple of weeks and have spent the rest of my life between Cheshire and the Isle of Man. No doubt this accounts for my ardent loyalty to Lancashire, my Yorkshire attitude to spending money, my Cheshire accent and my adherence to the Manx slogan "Traa delore" (time enough), which can be translated as "'Never put off until tomorrow what you can do the day after that".

A QUICK history lesson.

The FA came into being during 1863, some 14 years before the first Wimbledon, the first Test Match against Australia and General Custer and his men received a hiding from Crazy Horse and his Red Indian Braves at the Little Big Horn Stadium.

How many people know when the first floodlit football match was played? You could win a few euros with this one. Fans generally say the famous Wolves versus Honved match or similar contest in the 50s, but as a Lancastrian the answer hurts a bit. The City of Sheffield (yes, in Yorkshire) hosted a match at Bramall Lane played under the light cast by arc lamps in September 1878, although Lancashire got a bit of pride back later the same month by putting on the first floodlit Rugby match when Broughton took on Swinton. At that time the teams changed ends every time a goal was scored, there was no heading and throw-ins were one-handed, the throw going to the first team to touch the ball after it went out of play. That's how the word 'Touchline' came into being, a term that has stayed with us ever since. These gems of little-known information are revealed in an attempt to set the scene for some insight into my family connections and their perhaps small but significant contribution made to the shaping of Association Football in general and the professional game in particular.

In those early years Scottish teams came to Lancashire for 'friendlies' and the Scots, who had been known to receive money for playing, were impressed by the job opportunities and the relatively high standards of living in the North West of England. This led to some of them moving to the locality with the prospect of better wages and the chance of playing for some emerging and exciting clubs.

The idea of professionalism was severely frowned upon, particularly in the old school tie areas of the South, don't you know? It seems like déjà vu, but the FA ducked out of the responsibility of carrying out specific investigations. Lancashire clubs could see no valid reason against professionalism, particularly as there were professional cricketers already earning their livings from sport. They forced the issue and eventually, in 1885, the authorities of the day made professionalism legal in Association Football.

This was soon after the two-handed throw, neutral referees – previously two umpires, one from each club – and just before the penalty kick was introduced at the suggestion of the Irish FA. There must be a funny there somewhere, but I can't think of a politically correct one.

Just to tidy up the quick history lesson, it may interest you to know that it was not until 1894 that the referee was given complete control of the game. Prior to this decisions, as in cricket, were only given on the appeal from players, and that mind-shattering piece of information opens up all kinds of hilarity when you consider the antics and fatuous appeals of some of today's prima donnas.

The Football League was formed in Manchester during 1888 and there wasn't a Southern club to be seen. The original twelve clubs consisted of six from Lancashire; Accrington, Blackburn Rovers, Bolton Wanderers, Burnley, Everton and Preston North End and six from the Midlands; Aston Villa, Derby County, Notts County, Stoke, West Bromwich Albion and Wolverhampton Wanderers.

Recently my friend Brian Warburton gave me a newspaper article written by a man of the cloth talking about the Church's effect on several teams in England. In fact, there are many clubs who owe their existence to the influence and direction of the Church, two examples in Lancashire being St. Domingo's (Everton) and St. Mark's (Manchester City). Despite its strong religious connections, Manchester United started life as the Lancashire and Yorkshire Railway Company Football Club, eventually running into financial problems, as did several other clubs, including City, and being saved from extinction by four businessmen, all British – not a Glazer or an -ovich in sight – investing £500 each. In 1902, after considering the names Manchester Celtic or Select, the club, which was then known as Newton Heath, settled for Manchester United. City's name evolved by way of St. Mark's, West Gorton and Ardwick, with, over the years, many Directors, managers and players being Masons; hence the traditional Sky Blue and White playing strip. This led to associations with Glasgow Rangers and Everton among others, although Joe Mercer once told me that things reversed on Merseyside around the time of the Second World War.

To my knowledge, generally this never created any problems between the Manchester clubs, although United have always had the first pick of the Catholic youngsters, even those who supported City. One United legend, a friend and contemporary of mine and who shall remain nameless, said he learned his football kicking a tennis ball against the walls of City's Maine Road Stadium, but played for United, though the first result he looked for when he finished playing was City's.

My family always maintained it didn't matter a monkey's toss what colour, creed or nationality a player was born into, providing he was proud to pull on a City shirt. As a club we were early among those who encouraged black local lads, while a controversial signing after the Second World War was that of the former German paratrooper Bert Trautmann. When he first played there was a boycott by some of the club's Jewish supporters, but within weeks and Bert's rave notices in the papers they came back into the fold. Bert eventually received an Honorary OBE in the Queen's Honours List. It's hard to imagine people protesting about the arrival of a foreigner now as the situation has gone to the other extreme in recent times and an English or British name is something of a rarity, especially in the Premiership. Not much scope for our youngsters in the modern era, but more about that later.

My father grew up in stables as his father (my grandfather) was a carriage proprietor and ran the horse buses, hansom cabs and charabancs around Manchester and into the nearby countryside at the weekends. He became renowned for ferrying the visiting football teams to the city from the stations to whichever ground they were playing at and there is one famous tale of him sweeping along the highway from Bury Football Ground to Victoria Station in Manchester in such haste that it was a white-faced Newcastle United team that staggered from their seats at the end of the journey.

Grandpa was only some 5' 5" tall, but as tough as nails and there are family legends of how he ruled the drivers with his fists if necessary, bearing in mind the drivers were no shrinking violets. I bore some witness to this motivational technique. He used to shake his fist at me and say "Give 'em socks" to gee me up. He also had a magical way of producing sweets from his ears and nose which endeared him to this small boy. He was a Justice of the Peace and a Manchester Councillor and several times passed up the opportunity to be Lord Mayor of Manchester, believing the fact that he left school at 13 possibly made him short on the educational standards. When I consider some of the recipients in later years I think perhaps he underestimated himself. In fact his manners, demeanour and experience – including twelve months spent in Philadelphia, America, at the age of 18 – earned him great respect not only in Manchester, but throughout football. To quote from the *Manchester Evening News* of September 1950:

'Celebrating his 83rd birthday today is Mr A.E.B. Alexander, one of the few remaining Grand Old Men of football who link us with the early days of the game as we now know it. As well respected in the City as he is at Lancashire Cricket Club headquarters, every football ground in the country and at Gatley Golf Club, Mr. Alexander keeps up an active interest in sport and is always ready to give forthright views on soccer. "I'd pay them what they're worth and not a penny more" is one of his favourites.

In a lifetime full of incident and memories Mr Alexander likes to recall two assignments which came to him early in the century, when he was a carriage proprietor in Manchester. In 1904, when City won the Cup at Crystal Palace, he met the victors at the station and drove them round Manchester with the Cup. Five years later at their special request he drove Manchester United's Cup-winning team to Clayton for a League match with Woolwich Arsenal, who followed behind in another carriage-and-four, also provided by him.'

My grandfather is unique in as much as he was a founder, President, Chairman, Vice-Chairman, Director and Manager of City. He fought shy of the Chairman's position, quoting the same reasons as for the Lord Mayor's job and saying he was a players' man and that was his value to the club. That same sentiment was carried by Dad and myself during our football lives as the Alexander family's influence continued at the club for over a century.

Both he and my maternal grandfather were involved in the founding of Manchester City, although Grandpa William stayed in the background as a supporter. However, I'm told both sides of the family used to meet up on Sundays and replay the previous day's match.

But for someone like Grandpa Albert to become manager required some individual circumstances. In 1926 City were in dire straits and heading for relegation to the Second Division. The Manager, David Ashworth, departed and Grandpa was asked to take on the job. He agreed, but would remain in post only until a permanent replacement was found. It is recorded that he mounted a mini recovery, and, although it was too late to save City from the drop, the team reached the FA Cup final at Wembley, losing to Bolton Wanderers in a Lancashire Derby. The final was played on the Saturday following the birth of a baby to the Duchess of York, a little girl who would become our Queen Elizabeth II. We are lucky enough to still have photographs of Grandpa introducing her grandfather King George V to the team before kick-off.

Many are the tales concerning my Grandpa Albert golfing up to the age of 86 and several anecdotes on prison visiting, something he firmly believed in. I really don't know how true this one is, but he always reckoned that in the last match he himself played in the players, gentlemen all, wore top hats and long trousers. A true gentleman throughout, he was proud of the transfer he organised for full-back Bert Sproston to come to City from Spurs just before World War II for a record fee of £10,000. So, if like me you are looking for people to impune for the ridiculous transfer market of current times, we can lay some of the blame at the feet of my grandfather, Old Albert.

Germans loomed large in the early 20th century for most British people and none more so than my grandfather. City's tour of Germany in 1937, celebrating that season's first ever League Championship victory, had one or two unusual facets. According to Grandpa, the players were instructed by the authorities to give the Nazi salute during the German national anthem, but refused and simply stood to attention as for any normal anthem. The other surprise was that the Germans had smaller balls than us (probably why we beat them in two World Wars) and they insisted they were used for the games. However a compromise was agreed and half a match was played with the English ball and half with the German-sized one.

During the German Blitz on Manchester at Christmas 1940 my grandparents were bombed out of their home and came to live with us, unfortunately Grandma dying three months later, but Grandpa lived with us for his remaining twelve years, obviously giving me the opportunity to know and understand him far better than would normally have been the case. Mention of bombing and so on, it makes one wonder in these politically correct days if I could sue the German Government for damages as the Luftwaffe blew me out of bed and covered me with broken glass as my 1940 Christmas present?

Mention of the 'bomb business' reminds me of the recent occasion when, under orders "It's about time you tidied up the garden shed", I found, among other things, a war-time programme, price one penny, single sheet of recycled paper for the Manchester City versus Crewe Alexandra game on Whit Monday, 13 May 1940. The following is printed under the formation layout which used to be the normal presentation of a teamsheet:

AIR RAID PRECAUTION

In the event of a WARNING being given all EXIT GATES will immediately be opened and the spectators on the popular side are asked to make their way to the Grandstand and take shelter.

DO NOT CROSS THE PLAYING PITCH as this will only cause congestion, and above all,

BRING YOUR GAS MASK. This is imperative.

The City Programme Editor did not think much of the proposal to decide the Championship of each section by goal average or percentage and not on points in the new season. However, this would enable a comparison to be drawn between clubs who did not manage to play the same number of matches, and that ended up being pretty much everyone as many clubs struggled to field teams. It seems to have been a reasonable idea to me, as they were never sure that a fixture could take place right until kick-off under war time conditions, with travel restricted and passes out for players from their barracks like golddust. For instance the coming season would see Manchester United's ground at Old Trafford bombed out of first team use for some seven years.

If you are interested, the following teams constituted the League North A for 1940/1941: Blackburn Rovers, Blackpool, Bolton Wanderers, Everton, Liverpool, Manchester United, Preston North End, Stoke City, Wolverhampton Wanderers, Burnley, Bury, Manchester City, Accrington Stanley, Barrow, Chester, Crewe Alexandra, New Brighton, Oldham Athletic, Port Vale, Rochdale, Southport, Stockport County, Tranmere Rovers and Wrexham.

I did warn that you could become a mine of useless information, didn't I?

Another quirk of fate, I picked up a piece of paper from the same bag of long-forgotten papers in the shed and discovered a letter from the then City Chairman to Dad, thanking him for his work on behalf of the 'A' team during the season that had just concluded. It was dated 13th May 1924.

IN 1951 Grandpa Albert was honoured by the Lancashire Football Association by being promoted to Vice-President. This would prove to be about the only thing at which I got the better of him, apart from the occasional game of snooker and golf, as I was made up from Vice-President to Life Vice-President. He and I being the only ones to receive such honours in the history of Manchester City Football Club.

It was reported in 1953 that 'the football family Alexander had sweated it out continuously for football and Manchester City since it was West Gorton, before it was Ardwick and before it became Manchester City in 1894. With the death this week of Albert, Alexander the First, football in this country has lost one of its most colourful characters. He was well known to thousands of players and officials in the Boardrooms of every club in Britain. It might almost be said that Mr Alexander WAS Manchester City. He strode gingerly into the World as a greengrocer's errand boy at four shillings and sixpence a week and then his rapidly expanding ideas culminated in the pilgrimage to America. Another important date was his entry into the carriage hire business, which entailed driving Football League teams to grounds all over Lancashire in horse drawn vehicles.'

Originally my grandfather was known as Albert Alexander senior and my father Albert Alexander junior which mutated into 'Old Albert' and 'Young

Albert' and then I think probably it was Manchester City manager Joe Mercer who christened Dad 'Little Albert'. At the time my father was known as Albert junior and his ambitions lay in the direction of a possible career in either professional football or cricket, both games at which he was blessed with considerable talent. His first recorded engagement for Manchester City was in 1900 at the age of 8, when he had the job of showing the Committee and guests to their seats in the stand.

When the First World War erupted in 1914 Dad went out to France and spent four years in the trenches, where in 1918 he suffered injuries in a gas attack. He recovered, but had to give up any hopes of a playing career in professional sport, although he became a capable golfer, a game he enjoyed right up to the end of his life.

He rarely spoke of his wartime experiences except sometimes when the family of one of his Army pals came round to our house for Sunday tea. The two men retired to the lounge and I was allowed to listen, entranced, to some of their reminiscences. Hardly surprisingly, Dad was not overly keen on Germans and in later life, on hearing some of the atrocities he came across, I could understand his feelings. He mellowed a bit and was quite friendly with the President of Hertha Berlin when we played them. I have a photo somewhere of Dad as Chairman of City and this other chap, whose name I forget, standing side by side. The Hertha President was reputed to have been one of Hitler's bodyguards. You may recall these giants in black uniforms and black steel helmets, who stood outside the door of Hitler's Chancellory Offices, well this guy certainly fitted that bill as he was about 6' 10" tall and my father 5' 5". Talk about the long and short of it. He seemed decent enough, though, and I still have a cigarette lighter that he gave me with 'Hertha BSC' engraved on it.

But Dad was never one to hold personal grudges for xenophobic reasons. He was close with Bert Trautmann when he came to City and over forty years after he finished playing, Bert and I are still good friends.

My father was introduced to many famous people in his time, unlike my grandfather who met many infamous ones in his position of prison visitor and an execution witness. Dad sat with Royalty and many foreign dignitaries as well as being totally comfortable among everyday supporters of any club. During my time, I met Royalty, Presidents, Prime Ministers, Tribal Chiefs (principally in

Scotland and Australia) and celebrities, some of whom I recall later in appropriate context. A claim to this type of fame is meeting Princess Margaret on one occasion and being surprised to find how tiny she was in real life. There is a photo in this book of my receiving a replica of the FA Cup from HRH The Duke of Kent at the Football Association Centenary Dinner in which I am about to receive and return the mystical handshake.

The advantage of growing up in this type of situation helps you to be a little less in awe of authority, although I like to think that I am perhaps more respectful. I will never forget a Station Warrant Officer in the RAF on an occasion when I was an Officer Cadet and chosen to be the 'stick man' or lackey to the Air Officer Commanding on an Inspection Day. He told me not to worry, but I cannot repeat his somewhat indelicate comparison that implied that all men are equal in certain basic circumstances.

Realising his playing days were over, Dad organised and started a City 'A' or third team in 1919 to develop young local players, something which would become a life-long passion of mine, and stayed as manager, coach, selector, chauffeur and general dogsbody, all on a voluntary basis, with no expenses, until he was co-opted on to the Board of Directors in 1958. Thereby hangs a tale. Despite his longstanding connections to City, in 1941 he was invited to join the Board of Manchester United. Although he was very flattered Dad said he was 'dyed Blue' and could not change. After the Munich air disaster of February 1958, approaches were made again, but City got wind of the situation and immediately co-opted him on to the Board, which at that time was somewhat geriatric and in not too good health.

Had my father taken up the kind offer it is fascinating and frankly mind boggling to imagine what the consequences could and would have been for both City and United. I might even have been the Chairman of Manchester United and become a millionaire. On the other hand, either or both Dad and I could have been victims of the Munich disaster. Life deals out some funny cards.

By the kind courtesy of the United Board, my father and I had our own seats in the Directors Box and a special car park pass to Old Trafford and usually went there mid-week or whenever City had no game. It used to be good for a laugh as I drove over the crowded bridge towards the car park and right among the heaving masses heading for the game. Someone would see his distinctive bowler and the shout would go up "There's Albert", "Come to see a decent team, Albert?" and so on. Dad would beam and doff his hat to the supporters, who generally cheered or waved back to us. What a wonderful atmosphere. Would that the World were like that today.

Once, towards the end of his life, before I dropped him off at his home after a weekly Board Meeting, he commented "You know, I think I've seen the best of it all. I don't really envy you, Son, but do your best and try to keep some dignity". I have never forgotten that remark.

FOR YEARS Dad wrote a brief account of each City A team match, including goalscorers, players expenses and referees' performances for the weekly meeting of Directors. I still have two suitcases full of reports from 1919 to 1958. From them I have learned how Dad developed many youngsters who became famous players during their careers, two examples being Matt Busby and Frank Swift. Dad decided Matt was not quite quick enough to really exploit his talents as an inside-forward, where he initially played, and moved him back to wing-half, from which position Matt never looked back, playing many years for City, Liverpool and captaining Scotland. Their friendship made the links between Manchesters City and United very strong once Matt was appointed as the manager at bombed out Old Trafford at the end of the Second World War. United had camped out at Maine Road while their ground was rebuilt throughout 1946. Not that this ever dented the fierce inter-club rivalry of course, but that was an era when you could do battle on the pitch and then have a drink together afterwards. The pressures were far less intense.

Dad persevered with goalkeeper Frank Swift, a former Fleetwood fisherman who went on to become a football legend. He had huge hands, an 11¾ inch span, and my father encouraged him to throw the ball out to his own players as a quick set up from defence to attack. This ploy was novel at the time and Frank's throws became prodigious and we all know now how goalkeepers have thrown the ball for years. Not one to say much about himself, Dad did on one rare occasion reveal to a Press man that he had always had faith that Frank would make it to the top one day, despite the doubts of many others. He said, "Frank let in a lot of goals, but I said 'he'll make it, you see'". Then he said, "I went to an England versus Scotland International one time. Frank Swift was in the England goal and Matt Busby the Captain of Scotland". He permitted himself a smile. "Two of my boys".

Matt remained a friend of our family from those days until his death. On the occasion of the FA Cup final in 1969, when City met Leicester, we invited all living members of our previous Cup final teams, which at that time included Matt from the 1934 side. During the course of the Celebration Banquet at the Cafe Royal in London, Matt was in the Gents' toilet next to a friend of mine, Harry Finlaison, whom he knew. He said, "Hello Harry, a great night. I'm so pleased for Albert, I'm just so pleased for Albert."

'It is indeed desirable to be well descended but the glory belongs to our ancestors.'

My parents were Victorians; 'with it' in some ways, but still Victorians and although there was love aplenty, very little emotion was evident in most circumstances. I remember passing the entry exam for Manchester Grammar School, quite an achievement if I say so myself, and Dad told me many years later how thrilled they were, but at the time he simply said "Good shot". I always had the feeling that people were surprised when I managed to do something well. For instance, by nine years of age I spoke pretty decent French, was fluent at twelve and not bad at German by fourteen yet I can't recall anybody, except perhaps my sister, commenting and she probably wanted to borrow something.

I went to the College of Art and then to the Royal Air Force where I was in my element. An embryonic birdman since wartime childhood, I was doing something I really enjoyed and made Flying Officer before completing my service. Again some surprise at home, although they knew I had no problems with getting my hands, knees and face dirty. I'd loved playing Cowboys and Indians (the Native American variety) shooting and fighting people – in fact all the attributes that could be required these days to produce an unsociable thug complete with ASBO. Of course, as a boy I had shot down hundreds of German and Japanese aeroplanes during the War, that fantasy assisted by having two actual pilots, a navigator and an air gunner in the family.

I returned home after national service to the expectation of becoming an Assistant Professional Golfer or pro Footballer. Wages were virtually peanuts at golf and £12 a week plus £2 win and £1 draw during the season for the top footballers. There was the opportunity to follow Dad into the cardboard and paper trade, but I had trained as a commercial artist and that was where I settled, enjoying the next sixteen years with the publicity branch of the National Coal Board.

Frankly, there was by no means any certainty that I would have made it at either sport and Dad's comment that I could enjoy and give anybody a decent game of golf and, as far as football was concerned, I would be better off in the commercial world and perhaps getting the odd banknote in my shoe on a Saturday afternoon set the pattern for my future.

Another facet of life that no doubt shaped my character was that my family was decimated in the decade 1951 to 1961 as, with the exception of Mum and Dad, I lost all my immediate family to flying tragedies and incurable illnesses. My mother was heartbroken, but kept up appearances for the rest of her life. Dad was deeply affected but showed little on the surface having witnessed many of life's injustices. Supposedly I became a survivor, taking the foibles, good times and the pitfalls with a philosophy and hardness it is doubtful I would otherwise have shown or accepted.

A brother-in-law who was a test pilot was killed in an accident and on the evening after his funeral, along with my team-mates at Styal FC, I received Cup Winner and League Championship medals and was informed that Bob Skewes, my left-wing partner, and myself had been the subject of enquiries by Manchester United's legendary chief scout, Louis Rocca. Some hilarity ensued in both camps when it was discovered who I was and anyway I already figured on City's books. Louis and Dad were friends and I'm told there was some leg pulling among the rivals. Bob had done his National Service and in his early twenties was too old for serious consideration by top pro clubs even in those days. Surprising really, as a year later my last game before going into the Air Force was at the time of the Stanley Matthews FA Cup final of 1953 and within two months of my twentieth birthday I was the youngest member of City's A team, which included some players in their mid-twenties with first team experience. A bit different from today.

I started life as a centre-forward – didn't we all? Probably it was because my grandfather and father taught me to use left and right feet to kick a ball almost as soon as I could walk, saying that I would never be any good at football unless I could use both feet, even now I can say honestly that I really do not know which is my natural foot. I wish I could say the same of many modern day professional footballers.

I came across an interesting theory when attending a pre-commissioning medical at the Air Ministry when I was twenty. I was asked by the eye specialist if I wrote left or right-handed. Writing and drawing were done by my right hand, but anything else was either picked up or done with the nearest hand – very useful for hammers, paintbrushes and screwdrivers among other things. The eye man explained his question by saying that both my eyes were of equal strength, 20/20, and in most cases people had one eye stronger than the other and used the corresponding hand and foot as natural. You can learn something new every day . . . stick with me, folks, and you will become a mine of useless information. I have always been grateful for having good eyesight and even now – in my 70s – do not wear glasses, even for reading, although when watching televised matches and listening to the commentaries and comments by some 'experts' I often find myself wondering if I've missed something.

There has always been a shortage of left-sided players at all levels – it wasn't just a malaise of the nineties and noughties – so, being so blessed, I played most of my football at left-half, inside-left or left-wing. It's a good job I did otherwise I just might be writing this book on stamp collecting or netting butterflies. Strangely enough, some time after Dad died, Eric Todd of *The Guardian* told me that Young Albert had always fancied my chances as a tough left full-back. For the benefit of any younger readers, that was the player with a British name who played in front of the goalkeeper, had a number 3 on his shirt which under no circumstances whatsoever was removed until taking a shower after the game.

I used to dread Dad watching me play. Mostly he would be off at some more important first team game, but he did sometimes sneak a look and would tell me some time later about my failings and occasionally any good points. I suspect Eric Todd was exaggerating somewhat, although I have often wished Dad was around to have debated the point. How many of us find out things when it is too late to do anything about them? Only playing one season at school, much to the displeasure of 'Chang' Lund, the master in charge of football at Manchester Grammar, I was playing in open age football at 15 against works teams like British

Driver Harris, ICI and so on. I mention this simply to point out that this cannot happen in the modern, sophisticated and politically correct world where lads of that age are not considered suitable to mix it with so-called adults. We used to get abused by the adults all right, but it was with nothing worse than a boot up the backside and there were ways and means of getting your own back on the blind side of the referee.

Gatley Football club had played Sunday friendlies for a couple of years against teams like the exiled Polish Forces team, the Maccabi and similar ethnic teams, I suppose you would call them today, who were not playing in any particular league as a team but supplied players for various clubs on Saturdays. As one of the founding members of Gatley (Gatley Gunners, because the only shirts we could buy at that time were Arsenal red and white ones) I was thrilled to play in our opening league game, my great pal Jim Burns scoring the equalising goal and me scoring the winner. I had to put up with a great deal of leg pulling about mis-hitting the shot which kidded the goalkeeper by default, so to speak, but I managed the last laugh when the Press published a photograph taken from behind the goal showing me belting the ball and the keeper going the wrong way.

But the media didn't always work for me. I scored what I considered my best ever goal – a late equaliser in a vital match – with a really satisfying shot from just outside the penalty box, and spent all week looking forward to reading about it in the Stockport Advertiser or Express when the papers came out on the following Friday. The girls who followed the team all read these papers and I thought I'd be a hero, with the obvious perks to follow. What happened? I quote from the cutting still retained 'Gatley equalised with a tremendous rising drive from outside the penalty area'. I was mortified. No mention of my name?!

The other good goal I scored but missed seeing was on a Boxing Day when I was 30-odd years old and had played for some years in the annual charity match for one pub against another (before the breathalyser, of course). Players wore a selection of gear from pyjamas and top hats to the keen operators parading in shorts and real boots. I scored one from about 30 yards and was told it went in like a rocket. Unfortunately I didn't see it as I was lying flat on my back staring at the sky, in what felt like six inches of stinking mud having lost my footing when striking the ball. Ah well, such is life and such was life before TV cameras, instant replays and pundits telling you what you should have seen. Two great moments denied me.

What part does the weather play in our National game? Hardly anybody ever considers this intriguing question. Pitches undoubtedly stand up to the weather better than they did a few years ago, but British football is played in everything from blazing sunshine to mist, snow, pouring rain and gales. Many of the foreign, or is it non-British, players who make up most of the Premiership have only played in continual heatwave conditions rather than a Middlesbrough drizzle or a blizzard in Stoke-on-Trent, whilst homegrown players have to contend and mature with the vagaries of the British climate. These days you see players wearing gloves, thermal undershorts and vests, usually displaying well-rewarded advertising, which are exposed when the shirt is ripped off, despite the imminent yellow card, after scoring a goal.

Still, I'm pleased to see that FIFA have come down on that one and made it a Yellow card offence if a player removes his shirt in celebration, in some cases exposing his tattoos and in some others possibly getting a few spectators of both sexes mildly excited. Some of the after-goal celebrations these days look like an All Blacks versus Australia rugby scrum and you wonder how the players don't hurt themselves when you consider how easily and regularly some of them go down in apparent agony after the least bit of a tackle.

At one point of my time in the Royal Air Force I was the Sports and Athletics Officer at RAF Hednesford, a station in the Midlands where many well-known sportsmen were posted and we had tennis, rugby, soccer, swimming and cricket stars, apart from the usual Forces quota of self-proclaimed sexual athletes. Many of the sportsmen were already professionals and household names, others came on to the scene on completion of their National Service, which at that time was two years. Derek Ibbotson, the international runner, was one I had in the Station cross country team and years later we met up at City when he was the Puma area representative.

A similar situation existed from the Army angle at the Royal Army Ordnance Corps depot at Donnington, where they also had a good football team, including the likes of Welsh international Mel Charles and later a certain Robert Charlton, who looked as though he might make a bit of a player.

I met John Charles many years later when City played Juventus and certainly he came across as the revered 'Gentle Giant' whereas his brother Mel in my experience was as hard and tough a player as you could wish to avoid.

At the end of 2000 former England cricket captain Colin Cowdrey died and Ian Wooldridge wrote a piece about his illustrious career as one of England's cricketing greats, mentioning the fact that Colin, on returning from an outstanding cricket tour of Australia, had been conscripted into the RAF for his National Service. After a couple of weeks he was medically discharged with 'flat feet' and went on to pursue his career as a cricketer for many very successful years. At the time, much was made of his missing out on his National Service for physical reasons when everybody realised he was a World class sportsman, although there were fitness reasons that the layman probably either did not know about or understand. Colin came under some very unfair criticism on this topic and Ian said in his article that the cricketer had suffered some unhappiness throughout his life because of this incident.

I felt it was the right thing for me to drop a line to the well-respected journalist and mention that I had been the Sports Officer when Cowdrey was due to be posted to RAF Hednesford for his basic training and we were getting very excited thinking we would murder all the other cricket opposition with the runs this man was bound to score for us. I made the important point that when he was discharged there was no ill-feeling among his comrades or superiors and whilst we were disappointed he would not be playing for us we hoped he would continue to do his bit for cricket and England in particular.

Another of life's coincidences followed the next Saturday morning at my Golf club when somebody commented that Ian Wooldridge had mentioned me in that morning's paper on the subject of Colin Cowdrey. I had not had the chance to look at the papers before going out and I explained to my golfing mates what it concerned. Terry Beatson, a retired orthopaedic specialist and one time RAF surgeon said, "And I was the man who examined and medically failed him. No problems, but a bit different with another England player when I was put under some pressure by the Cricket Authorities."

Sometimes it is an unfair world. I don't know who it was but I seem to remember somebody once commented that the public do not know enough to be experts, yet know enough to decide between them.

In July 1950 Dad outlined a plan in the Press which he'd had under consideration for over twenty years and thought worthy of investigation by football's legislators. He had not submitted his ideas before because he felt so many clubs were over cautious in financial matters and could not – or would not – pay their players more than was absolutely necessary. He realised that although the best solution would be for clubs to pay a player what he is worth to them, such a scheme would be impractical and would lead to jealousy between the haves and the have nots. Don't laugh at these figures and remember a general national wage was about £3 in 1950 and five years later I joined the Coal Utilisation Council in quite a responsible position and was paid under £8 a week. If you did well, you had an annual merit rise of £50 per year and in the late 50s I couldn't believe my luck when I had one rise of £100 a year, i.e. an extra £2 a week, so footballers really weren't too badly paid at that time.

Briefly Dad proposed a minimum wage of £8 for the Third Division clubs, £10 for the Second and £12 for the First. These wages should then be increased by annual increments over a period of five years until the maximum of £12, £16 and £20 respectively. Naturally these figures were purely hypothetical and were submitted as a basis for discussion among clubs who could adjust them to suit their own finances. Summer wages, which at that time were less than during the season, would be fixed proportionately.

Dad's main argument was that the prospect of a higher wage the following season – providing the club felt that it had been earned – would act as a deterrent to a player's desire to join another club. For example, should a First Division player qualify for a maximum wage of £20 per week he would not wish to join another club in the same Division and start at the minimum. In the same way, a player on the maximum Second Division wage seeking a transfer to the First Division would realise it would take him a year or so to qualify for the wage he was already getting. The overall object was to encourage players to remain loyal and earn higher pay at their current club by their own endeavours. As far as other benefits were concerned, he suggested a £1,000 'loyalty bonus' after five years, which would have bought a house and a car, a further £1,250 after ten years and if the player qualified through loyal service for a third benefit he would receive £1,500.

As it was commented in the newspapers at the time, 'naturally some clubs will be horrified at the thought of having to pay out more money in wages and benefits, but sooner or later the day will dawn and if they want the results and to control the inflation of the transfer market, they will have to consider this scheme or something similar.'

With the recent re-emergence of Chelski from the catacombs of Stamford Bridge, the old adage apparently is still true:

> '*There is no fortress so strong that money cannot take it.*'

A typical example of how situations can be intentionally or unintentionally misrepresented is illustrated by the following extract from a letter I wrote to the Sports Editor of the *Daily Express*, at the time of the final game to be played at Maine Road in May 2003 when people were asked for their outstanding memories of the ground. Broadcaster Stuart Hall claimed to have quelled a massive mob, demanding the appointment of a new manager, outside the ground on Good Friday 1965 by confronting them after, in his words, 'the Chairman [my father] refused to go outside', and pacifying them by announcing the appointment to the posts of manager and coach of Joe Mercer and Malcolm Allison. This blatant untruth really got to my family and I was obliged to write to the Editor with the facts in order to set the unfortunate matter to rights, as any son would do for a father held in respect.

I refer to a statement attributed to Stuart Hall last Saturday in the article by Gideon Brooks. Having known Stuart for more than forty years, I am well aware of his sense of pomposity and melodrama but the serious nature of the concern of my family and myself at the slur on the name of my father, Albert Alexander the Chairman of Manchester City at that time, makes it fair that you should be in possession of the true details.

There was a demonstration outside the ground when several hundred disgruntled fans gathered and some threw coins, mainly heavy copper pre-decimal pennies at the windows of the club's offices and lounges. Would the police have tolerated an 8,000 strong brick-wielding riot mob?

A small splinter of broken glass hit my mother, which provoked my father, against the advice of the police, to go outside on to the main steps of the Club, which were open and not protected by a steel cage in those days. He held up his hands and when the jeering and booing died down said, "Have you people not got homes to go to? Please bear with us, we will get it right I promise you. Now get off home, the lot of you."

Little Albert was 72 years of age at that time. The police said it was a remarkable performance and the crowd dispersed without any further problems. My father went on to be certainly the most successful and probably the most popular Chairman in the history of the Club.

Hall's claim to have announced the appointment of the new managerial team at that time is also incorrect and if you are interested the true facts are as follows.

George Poyser resigned as Manager at Easter 1965 and City played out the season without replacing him. My father took ill in June and for confidentiality all enquiries from interested parties were given my ex-directory telephone number at my home in Heald Green. During that time I received calls from several household names including Liverpool manager Bill Shankly and Leeds boss Don Revie, who were both interested. However we went down a different route and so the destiny of those two gentlemen remained unaltered.

When Dad came out of hospital it was decided that Peter Doherty, one of the finest footballers ever to play for City, would be offered the job. However Peter was away on holiday and could not be located, even his sports journalist son, Paul, did not know his whereabouts and eventually it was agreed to appoint the second choice, Joe Mercer, who was unemployed at that time. Joe had a background of stress-related problems and when accepting the position of Manager he stipulated his need for a young coach, mentioning Malcolm Allison who had recently been sacked after a fallout with the Chairman of Plymouth Argyle and of whom probably nobody in Manchester had heard of at that time. These appointments were made in July 1965, some months after Hall's supposed announcement to quell the irate fans.

Distance lends enchantment, but you cannot alter facts. I leave it to you.

Yours faithfully
Eric Alexander

I was not expecting an apology, because we all know how "too late" they are in newspaperland, but I did consider an acknowledgement to me at my home, of my letter and confirmation Fax would be in order. Needless to say, no response was forthcoming. As they say:

> *'Journalists will happen, even in the best regulated families.'*

HALF-TIME

Without going into the whys and wherefores the City Board had been a little short on practical football matters for some time during the late 30s, 40s and early 50s and I have been reliably told by several sources over the years that the Directors were somewhat in awe of my father and his considerable knowledge and connections within the game. Without putting too fine a point on it, some of the Board were a little bit worried that the combination of Grandpa and Dad would put the rest of them rather in the shade and had come up with the unofficial principle that no more than one member of a family should be on the Board at the same time. Incidentally, this affected another family or two at the time but I don't think that had life-threatening consequences for the club, as it was more or less inheritance rather than background. Other clubs where this did not cause a problem come readily to mind, the Mears family at Chelsea, Kearns at West Ham, Robbins at Coventry, Hill-Woods Arsenal and Wisemans at Birmingham.

During the 1967/68 season a Director of Manchester City FC resigned and although there were no stipulated numbers regarding the constituency of the Board it created a vacancy. I discovered later that much as Dad would have liked me on the Board of Directors and felt that I could do a decent job on behalf of the club, he was very conscious of how it would look if he pressed for my appointment to go through and, after clearing the issue of two members of the same family being on the board with the other Directors, it was John Humphreys and Sidney Rose, and not Dad, who 'elevated me to the peerage' so to speak.

Obviously I was thrilled to bits to be invited to join the City Board and in those days it did not cross my mind what the public or the fans might or might not think about it, as that sort of thing was not controversial back page stuff but merely a few lines filling up space somewhere in the local papers.

Clubs have all sorts of personnel these days and I would not presume to discuss what Directors of football clubs know, do or contribute to the everyday running of what have become financial operations rather than a sporting environment, but when I joined City's Board each Director had an area of responsibility and was answerable to the full Board.

When I took up my place I was well aware that my position was to 'hear all, see all and say nowt', whilst getting the feel of things and until called upon to make a contribution to the proceedings. I was confident about my football knowledge and ability, but little did I appreciate at the time that among many other places, football would take me to the Acropolis, Aston Villa, Auschwitz and Bondi Beach, Bastogne and Bolton via Malta, La Scala Milan and Middlesborough to Waterloo. Wolverhampton, Ypres and Zabrze (can't recall anywhere starting with an 'X').

At the time John Humphreys was the Financial Director, while Sidney Rose, the eminent surgeon, looked after medical matters and I, directly following in my father's footsteps, became responsible for the Youth set-up, training facilities and the Maine Road pitch. Vice Chairman Frank Johnson was a solicitor and supposed to advise on legal matters, although the only time I asked him a question which would have protected City from any takeover, he gave me an answer which proved evasive, his reasons coming to light when he sold out his shares with the intent of starting a new life abroad.

I can't remember what Chris Muir was supposed to do, except that he seemed to diet on any food he could lay his hands on.

Other than Dad, I was the only Director who had played any serious football and that situation remained during the whole of my time in the capacity of Director and Chairman. It was fortunate for me that having been close to the action for a number of years prior to my joining the Board things fell into place without too much of a surprise. What was a little worrying was the blind, unquestioning faith some of my new colleagues appeared to have in the management and I wondered what they had achieved in order to become

Directors. I had always felt that some understanding of and expertise in football would be appropriate!

'Forty years on when afar and asunder' as it says in the football song 'how we look back and forgetfully wonder'. I don't forget and like most people who follow the game I do not wonder, when you can buy yourself virtually any position in the administration of football. That sounds a bit drastic, but that is how it appears to me from what I see, hear and read.

I prefer to believe:

> *'He that would eat the fruit must first climb the tree.'*

If you turn out to be no good, a lucrative 'goodbye and thank you' seems now to usually be on the cards. Things like that remind me that myself and my colleagues back in the 1960s had to pay our own petrol and expenses, other than hotel bills – and they were scrutinised to make sure we did not 'overdo' anything.

Of course in those days 'scoring' meant a goal and 'roasting' was a winger giving a full-back a torrid time.

SECOND HALF

A year or so after joining the Board of Manchester City, with my background and interest in bringing on the younger players and remit to develop the Youth side of the club, I decided to have a go at the Football Association coaching course. I realised this was taking a chance and leaving myself wide open to ridicule and leg pulling at best, but in for a penny, in for a pound and I was duly accepted.

The course was to last half a day per week for a couple of months or so and it was a bit daunting when on the first day you realised you were older and whilst fit, nothing like the standard of the others who numbered several internationals such as Nobby Stiles and Bill Foulkes in their midst. Denis Lowe, a journalist from the *Daily Telegraph* and with whom I had friendly eating contests over the years had also enrolled, but being a little bit overweight did not take much of a part in the practical events and I suspect that he mainly came along to find out how I performed. This thought made me try and ensure that I did not make a fool of myself and that earned me some respect. One incident sticks in my mind and I am reminded sometimes when players who should know better – and don't get me started on that one – argue with the referee over a decision. We were receiving a lecture on the Laws of the Game, prior to taking the Referees' examination, and the instructor, Maurice Somebody – and I apologise for not recalling your name, Sir – put a situation to us and asked if the decision was correct or wrong, asking for a show of hands. I was certain that I was right but no other hands went up. Bear in mind there were some fifteen or so professionals, including several internationals, in attendance. I thought 'Oh, Hell. This is where I feature in the

Telegraph as a total prat.' At that point I caught Nobby Stiles' eye and together we put up our hands.

We were the only two right and we had a relieved laugh about it afterwards, but it just goes to show how many players could, and probably still can, get themselves into problems by basic ignorance of the Laws. I managed to obtain the FA's Preliminary Badge and Certificate for Practical Coaching, Practical Performance, Coaching Method and the Laws of the Game. There was no way I wanted to become a full blown coach but I had proved something to myself which satisfied me. Recently, whilst looking for some programme notes made years ago, I came across a Football Association publication which shows that at the Manchester Professional Footballers' Coaching Course in 1969, four candidates were successful, Alexander, A.E., of Heald Green, Foulkes, W.A., of Sale, Metcalf, M., of Deeside and Stiles, N.P., of Stretford, so I had a brief moment of self satisfaction, rubbing shoulders, so to speak, with the famous. It was flattering that some time later Sir Matt Busby and I were appointed Joint Presidents of the Manchester Association of FA Coaches. It was interesting to see and hear how some of the others went about the course. Bill, for instance, reminded me of a Warrant Officer Drill Instructor I knew in the Air Force. Nobby, Bill and I got on well together, there was plenty of leg pulling and we have remained friends ever since. Bill was a very good golfer, highly competitive and, I believe, eventually went on to play for the County Team. He and I enjoyed several blood matches against each other for our respective Golf clubs.

Over the years, on behalf of the Lancashire Football Association, I have tested dozens of Referees during their promotion examinations and I have never forgotten my own feelings under those testing circumstances. It is a great pity that players who can earn, and I use the word 'earn' advisedly, millions of pounds per year cannot take the time or trouble, or be made as part of their contracts, to learn and properly understand the Laws of the game that they play. It would make a nice change to see certain players just get on with the game instead of performing 'The Dying Swan' or ranting at the referee, who more often than not doesn't sort them out and stamp his authority on the game.

IN THE good old days people talked about Soho in London, the Rieperbahn in Hamburg, or the Rue St Denis and Montmartre in Paris, but apparently the place to go in the late Sixties if an hour with Sweaty Betty, or her continental cousin, was your favoured evening's entertainment was Amsterdam (in fact it was available 24 hours a day in Holland I'm told!).

On this particular occasion City were playing Ajax and on the evening prior to the match John Humphreys, myself and another director, who shall remain nameless for reasons that will become apparent, went for a stroll around Holland's major city, taking in the sights and having the odd drink. For John and myself the activities were a purely academic exercise, but our colleague was one of those who giggled and looked surreptitiously at 'girlie magazines'. The 'ladies' of Amsterdam generally besport themselves in illuminated windows like shop frontages, displaying their wares and we had to wander past this one such window several times whilst colleague X was making up his mind.

Eventually I said, "For God's sake, if you are going to go in, go. We won't say anything and we'll wait for you over there in that bar."

Our 'hero' decided to have twopenny's worth and started up the six or eight steps at the front of the building, when suddenly lo and behold the door opened and who should start to come down the steps but a well-known professional footballer, who should have been in his (own) bed by this time. Humphreys and I were simultaneously speechless and spellbound, but from what we could see neither of the two customers gave any sign of their obvious recognition for each other, be it from short-sightedness or cold-bloodedness on the one part and temporary exhaustion on the other. The incident was never referred to again. Whilst I actually had no time for this particular director, to complete his stated task after such an encounter showed me he had, amongst other attributes, nerves of steel.

ANYONE CONNECTED with sport in any professional capacity will tell you that when things are not going well nobody wants to know you. Often difficult times also bring heavy criticism, usually without the author of such bile knowing the facts or reasons behind the problems. Conversely when things are good everybody wants a piece of the action. During the mid-Sixties when City were re-emerging, a group led by an advertising man, Peter Donoghue, attempted to buy into or buy out Manchester City. One of their number, a Scotsman Chris Muir, who once told me he was a shareholder of Heart of Midlothian, was the only one who knew anything about the game and eventually to placate the group and in an endeavour to be democratic the Directors invited him onto the Board. Muir was a Labour Councillor for some Manchester Ward.

It was stipulated at the time that Chris would be the one and only appointment which would be made from the consortium, but during my first year on the Board Muir made it obvious that he would be proposing his friend, Manchester solicitor Michael Theodore Horwich, for the Board at the next Annual General Meeting. It was made very plain to Muir that this man would be totally unacceptable to the Board and Frank Johnson was particularly adamant on this subject.

Against the wishes of the Board, Muir proposed Horwich and naturally he was not elected. At a special Board Meeting Muir was informed that he had gone against the specific instructions of his colleagues and he was formally requested to resign rather than suffer the indignity and embarrassment of being dismissed at an Extraordinary General Meeting. After blustering for some time he gave his verbal resignation and left the club. This was accepted and noted but a few days later, I imagine on the advice of his solicitor friend, Muir denied resigning and the matter went to the Courts of Justice. Embarrassing really for a football club, certainly in those days, to become involved in such a petty dispute. It was rank bad publicity, but I think where Chris was concerned, any publicity was good publicity.

John Humphreys used to say "Chris is a real politician, when things are going smoothly he has to introduce a glitch".

Anyway, the business went to Court. Apart from a couple of times as an Officer under Instruction in the RAF I had never been in a real Court and the week-long episode was hardly an enlightening experience. When you had been at the meeting and knew what had happened and what had been said, it was incredible how the legal eagles could twist things around.

'The first thing we do, let's kill all the lawyers.'
William Shakespeare

The Muir business was saddened somewhat when the Judge summed up on the Friday and said he would give his decision on the Monday and during the weekend the Counsel for City died suddenly. I think the Directors had been impressed by his work and attitude and perhaps it was a fitting tribute to him that we won the case comfortably and Muir went behind the scenes for some time, although he was to reappear during the Johnson sell out. Frank Johnson always maintained later that had he known Muir and Horwich were involved he would never have sold out whatever the consequences to himself and his future plans.

At the time of the Court events, Muir described manager Joe Mercer as "a joke", my father as "old Fashioned", myself as "a buffoon", John Humphreys' having his "sole interest based on his Umbro business", and Sidney Rose as "a chancer whose real ambition was to be on the Board at Manchester United."

I have known Sidney for over fifty years, he has helped me and I have helped him in many ways and we have always been good pals. Some have said that he tended to put his own interests first, but having witnessed some of the situations it would be difficult to make a criticism of him. Heading now, as he is, for ninety years of age he is still involved at City and good luck to him. Muir didn't comment on Frank Johnson.

As for my Dad being old fashioned, perhaps it was the bowler hat he often wore to matches.

THE TOUGH-TACKLING Alan Hardaker became Secretary of the Football League early in 1957 and began to make an impression when a few months later another Grand Old Man of football came into authority. This was another Yorkshireman, Joe Richards, who represented Barnsley Football Club and went on to become President of the Football League. Three years later the Football League Cup came into being, the brainchild of Joe and Alan, the three-handled Cup itself paid for out of Joe's own pocket and the original competition nicknamed by some sceptics as 'Hardaker's Folly'.

There was never any intention to rival or compete against the FA Cup, but much prejudice had to be overcome before the major clubs began to give this new competition some serious consideration. The advantage was that all finances stayed within the jurisdiction of the League.

Being the oldest competition in the world, the FA Cup had many years of tradition behind it and the final was always the biggest event in the English sporting calendar, a comment that is made without disrespect to other long-established sporting occasions. But in the late 1950s finance was coming more to the forefront of thinking in the game and the FA competition could be a disaster for some teams, both from financial and prestige angles when you consider it could mean playing – and sometimes losing – against amateurs, part time professionals, non-League and lower-League clubs. The arguments raged for some years with the competition gradually gaining support and recognition, but it was some seven years before all the Football League clubs, with the exception of the First Division Champions and the FA Cup Winners, joined up and the previously two-legged final was moved to Wembley Stadium. I believe that I am correct in saying that in 1970, when City and West Bromwich Albion met in the final, it was the first year that all 92 League Clubs entered.

I cannot recall if Joe Richards lived long enough to see the huge success of his brainchild, but he did become Sir Joseph Richards and his competition has had some exotic and World famous names as sponsors, for what eventually became the acceptable Football League Cup competition.

As FA Cup winners, City entered the 1969/70 European Cup Winners' Cup competition and we had some interesting games in Spain, Belgium, Portugal and Germany before winning the final in Austria, as described later. However this abundance of success created some administrative problems, although they were the kind that brought a smile to the faces of any financially-orientated officials.

We flew out to Portugal to play Academica Coimbra at the beginning of March 1970, the game to be played on the Wednesday evening prior to our Saturday date at Wembley with West Bromwich. Not the ideal schedule, but sometimes success works against itself and the authorities don't always help matters by a lack of consideration, cooperation and a modicum of common sense. Not to mention quite an amount of jealousy in football, too.

The chartered British European Airways Trident was a new type and the pilot seemed determined to give us the benefit of some of its latest performance capabilities, including one of the quickest and steepest descents I could recall, apart from in my RAF days which was a different matter altogether. When we landed after the aforementioned descent just about everybody was a touch light-headed and staggered a bit crossing to the terminal. It could not have been the complimentary drink on board because Little Albert, a life-long teetotaller, said he felt a bit dizzy.

The hotel at Bussaco was a converted monastery with wonderful gardens and reputedly trees and shrubs from just about every country in the World. On the morning of the match, when we were to play Academica Coimbra, Joe Mercer, Harry Finlaison and I walked to the edge of the hilltop where the Duke of Wellington was supposed to have taken a look at the position of the Napoleonic troops of Marshal Ney and once again had that magical sensation of travelling in time. It's difficult to explain or to be understood by anybody not interested in such things, but I hope some of you will know the point I'm making. I have been very fortunate to have visited many historical sites during my lifetime, some off my own bat, so to speak, and some through my connections in various sports and the main thing in such circumstances, I believe, is to be grateful that life has afforded you such opportunities.

Not that it matters much so many years on, but we drew 0-0 and won the return leg 1-0. It had been considered a good idea to stay on overnight rather than travel back to Manchester very late, arriving home in the early hours of the Thursday morning. This would give the players a decent night's rest and a relaxing morning before the flight home prior to going down to London, as is said in the North, on the Friday in preparation for Saturday's League Cup Final.

However the return home was something of a disaster, brought on by snow and bad weather in England coupled with a baggage handlers' strike at Manchester Airport. I don't think it could have been inspired by any frustrated supporters of another well known local club as I seem to remember that the Chief Union man or Head Porter at that time was an ardent City man who looked after us very well when passing through the Airport. What should have been a comfortable two hour return finished up as a ten hour dose of drudgery, hardly ideal pre-match training for Wembley. The aeroplane was diverted to Birmingham, where we eventually arrived mid-evening and Secretary Walter Griffiths had managed to arrange a coach to meet us to transport the official party to the hotel in London where accommodation had hastily been confirmed.

Comments are sometimes made by both the football authorities and the members of the newspaper and journalistic professions about lack of cooperation between all parties and so on, but an example of the relationship held dear at that time by both the pressmen and our club was illustrated when all the newspaper men who had been on the trip used the airport telephone system (not exactly smoke signals, but no mobiles in those days), to contact their papers and to make their arrangements. The players and officials were seated on the coach and the newspaper lads arrived one by one until only Bob Russell of the *Daily Mirror* was missing. It turned out that he was having difficulty getting through both to his head office and his home, but everybody was tired, fed up with the extended travel and seemingly endless delays and some of the players started saying "Oh, leave him, let him make his own way", and "Come on, we've been at this all day. Let's get down there". Those are just a couple of the printable comments.

My father stood up at the front of the coach and said "All right, you've had your say and you did your job. Now Bob's trying to do his and we will wait for him. Somebody go and hurry him up, but we don't go without him."

Bob's colleagues told him later and he has never forgotten that typical performance of Little Albert.

We won the League Cup on a Wembley pitch that when we inspected it on the Friday, Joe Mercer described as a "cow patch". It had been covered with straw for protection against the frost and snow and really was bloody awful, but we won, so all was forgiven.

IN THE early 1900s when Grandpa had his carriage business there was a competitor firm in Manchester by the name of Williams. Apparently the rivalry did not end there as I was told the Williams family were United supporters.

The point is I had been riding motor bikes since I was sixteen and had always favoured 'Flat Twin' machines since seeing and hearing racing BMWs in the Isle of Man TT as a child in 1939. During the 60s I had bought Triumph cars from Williams, who in 1970 had become the main agents for the new BMW performance cars, which were relatively little known as opposed to the 'every yuppie has had one' culture of modern times. I asked the Managing Director of Williams if he could pull strings and get me a few days' loan of the latest BMW bike? This was fixed and shortly afterwards City got into the final of the European Cup Winners Cup, to play the Polish side Gornik Zabrze in Vienna. BMW and the kindly folk at Williams saw an opportunity to capitalise on the contact and asked if I would drive one of the new 2800 type cars to Austria and back at the time of the final. Ideally they wanted two, or preferably three, drivers to share the workload which would entail quite an impressive amount of time at the wheel and a testing average speed in order to make the trip in the time allotted and therefore the publicity worthwhile.

My two close friends, Alan Gordon and Harry Finlaison, along with myself, had between us driven motorbikes, cars, fire engines, tanks, lorries and flown aeroplanes, but most importantly had all driven extensively over Europe. Alan, Harry and their wives, together with my wife Mavis were going to the final and our three seats on the club-chartered aeroplane were given up to allow three paying guests the chance to travel with the official party to Vienna. Instead we were to drive to Southend and take the airborne car ferry across the Channel, before driving to Austria, calling at BMW Munich if we experienced any problems.

The match was to be played on the Wednesday evening, so we set off from Manchester at the crack of dawn on Monday morning in order to arrive in Vienna late afternoon Tuesday. We had decided to each drive in rotation for one hour at a time. I won't bore you with the details, but suffice to say that the other two, not being enthusiastic flyers, got a touch of the loose bowels when we saw and boarded the elderly converted DC4 car ferry.

We got to Koblenz before packing it in for the day, booked into a decent looking hotel and obtained three rooms next door to each other. This was rather fortunate as Alan and I were in our rooms getting ready to bathe and change when Harry shouted for us for some quick help (as you never know who might read this I won't use the exact words). We raced into his room to find him standing on a chair holding on to the main window, which was quite large. When he had tried to open it the frame had come away from its fittings and was now hovering some seventy or more feet above the main street of Koblenz, supported only by the rapidly tiring arms of one Harry Finlaison Esq., currently of Gatley, Cheshire, but should he let go probably to finish up for manslaughter as a cellmate of Rudolf Hess in Spandau. Unfortunately our well-known Goon-like sense of humour struck as Alan and I were rendered helpless with laughter, making what we thought were hilarious remarks whilst falling about on the floor in paroxysms, literally unable to move cogently enough to help him. To make matters worse, Harry then got the giggles himself and we had one hell of a job restoring the window to safety amidst the tears of laughter!

After a very enjoyable meal in an open air restaurant we moved on to a bar near the railway station, where there was a real mixture of clients. The word 'clients' is probably appropriate as there were several ladies of the night coming and going, as one might say. Alan could speak French, Harry reasonable Danish but I was the only one who could be understood in German and when a second round of beer arrived on the bar in front of us, just as we were about to move on, we wondered what was going on. We thought matters could get tricky, but it turned out that a customer at the end of the bar had bought the drinks for us as a goodwill gesture. It happened that he had been a German prisoner of war in the camp at Dunham, near Altrincham, only half a dozen miles from City's ground, although he did not know at the time of purchasing the close connection. He considered that he had received very good treatment and it was his way of saying "Thank you". Needless to say we had one or two more in his company before retiring after a long day.

Umbro and Adidas had come in to the car sponsorship and as the contact man John Humphreys suggested that as all was well and time on our side, Adi Dassler, founder of Adidas, would be pleased to see us at his house in Herzogenaurach, near Nuremburg. We diverted slightly to arrive at the Dasslers' in time for lunch. It was the first time I'd met Adi and we got along very well together. It was such a pity he died comparatively young. He and his brother had founded Adidas, although eventually they parted after a disagreement. The brother storming off to establish Puma in opposition. It makes you wonder what John Humphreys' father Harold, John himself for that matter, and Adi Dassler would make of the billions now floating around the sports world and the way the business is handled.

Harold and his brother founded Umbro (Humphreys Brothers) as a small manufacturing unit in Wilmslow and just like Topsy it grew and grew and grew. John died at just 49 years of age and soon afterwards the company was sold to an American outfit. This is a personal opinion, but I don't think either of the Humphreys would have been too keen on that conclusion.

Following a lovely meal we set off once again and, after experiencing rain, snow, sunshine and fog we arrived in Vienna in time for a clean up and an evening meal with our wives and the official party at the famous Sacha's restaurant, where those of you who remember Orson Welles's 1949 thriller *The Third Man*, set in

Vienna, was where Anton Karas played his famous zither Harry Lime Theme. We felt like conquering heroes arriving after a tumultuous journey, all expectant of a glorious fest. And what was the 'special' on the menu? . . . Boiled beef and carrots!

Hell's bells, I ask you. All the way from Lancashire, where the boiled beef and carrots are unsurpassed. I made do with extra beer instead.

A look next day at the famous horse academy and a trip to the Vienna woods occupied the day, and then we arrived at the Prater Stadium for the match. It was somewhat 19th century in design and mostly open to the elements, which did not smile kindly on the City fans and the half dozen or so Poles who slid under the Iron Curtain to support Gornik. Everybody got soaked, but we won so that made all the difference and trip worthwhile.

The next morning we set off early as we were booked on an evening ferry from Calais, allowing us to have a night's rest and a 'gentle' drive up to Manchester for the BMW Press reception in the early evening. All was going well until around lunch time when the autobahn suddenly became nose to tail with solid traffic. We could not understand what the problem was for some time until I asked another driver what was going on? Now, this was before Harold Wilson and his cronies decided the British should celebrate May Day and of course nobody in City's party had given a thought to the fact that on the Continent the First of May was a Bank Holiday.

We were stuck for hours and eventually managed to get off the autobahn and more by luck than good judgement contacted the AA. It was explained that there was no hope of progressing as we had arranged and they managed to secure us a berth on the ferry from Calais the following morning. We plodded on getting more and more weary as each hour session elapsed, until in the mid-evening somewhere in the middle of Belgium we decided to stop for a coffee and a sandwich. We were more or less in the countryside and pulled up at what looked like a roadside cafe. The waitresses looked rather 'exotic' and for three well-travelled men of the world it took a few moments for the penny to drop – or perhaps we were too tired to catch on. Had we been reporters from a well-known Sunday paper we would have 'made our excuses and left'.

As it was we drank our coffees, thanked the management for their offers of 'hospitality' and in the true spirit of entente cordiale left by being waved on our way by the staff.

I drove through the night as the other two fell fast asleep. This was well before the advent of the EU so Brussels in the middle of the night was as deserted as Aberdeen on a Flag Day.

A couple of hours' sleep in the night refreshed us for a dash to Dunkirk before the cafes were open so we could have a walk on the famous beaches to soak up the historic aura. Quite something.

We got back to England all right and having circumnavigated the London traffic we hit the M1 motorway north. I mention this because Harry was doing his hour and after the rigid lane discipline and positive driving on the Continent, the British standards were horrific. Alan and I both declared we were glad it was not our turn at the wheel.

We made it to the Press reception with about ten minutes to spare and changed just in time, although one or two sceptics reckoned we had hidden around a nearby corner to make the job look impressive. Joe and Nora Mercer, along with our wives, met us and it was a most enjoyable evening. It was a fascinating trip with a difference and one which has taken me almost as long to type as it did to drive to Vienna and back!

IN MAY 1970, a few days after completing the double of the Football League Cup and the European Cup Winners' Cup, City embarked upon a sponsored tour of Australia. The tobacco giants WH & DO Wills were the sponsors and I imagine there would be some raised eyebrows in today's politically correct and holier than thou world from the anti-nicotine brigade in learning this. But that was then . . .

Probably more importantly we were the guests of the Australian Soccer Federation who proved to be kindness itself and ensured the tour went smoothly and was enjoyed by all. You know, it is one thing to go on a close season or pre-season tour for commercial reasons or training purposes – hopefully both – but it can also be really enjoyable when the destination is interesting and the people go out of their way to be friendly and help you to explore their town, locality or country.

Director John Humphreys, secretary Walter Griffiths, manager Joe Mercer and coach Malcolm Allison led the party of sixteen players, well fifteen and a half really as Michael G. Summerbee had his ankle in plaster following an injury against Sheffield United. Mike had been an important cog in our wheel and we felt it was the right thing to do for him to come on the tour with us, where he could assist with the social arrangements. Francis Lee and Colin Bell were away with the England World Cup Squad in Mexico. As it happened John Humphreys could only get away from his business for the first couple of weeks, so Sidney Rose and I went out after the first week until the end of the trip.

Sidney and I had an unusual start to our journey down under via America, the BOAC VC10 taxied out towards the runway at Manchester Airport, halted and shut down engines. We were then unloaded along with the luggage from the holds which was stacked on the hardstanding alongside the plane. The Irish problems were in full swing at the time and there had been a bomb warning, so we all had to identify our own luggage before it could be reloaded and we were allowed to reboard the aeroplane. Some fellow travellers, I imagined, with damp underwear.

That reminds me of the time City returned from Belfast Airport after playing Linfield the previous evening. It was a scheduled flight and we all carried our own hand baggage. There was a lady security guard of uncertain years with an attitude that brought to mind that of Hattie Jaques' Matron roles in the *Carry On* films. She demanded that we all opened our hand baggage and started with Mike Summerbee, asking him to turn out the contents on to the counter. He rummaged around and delicately, between thumb and forefinger, held out to her the unwashed jockstrap he had worn during the match. She recoiled in horror (who would blame her?) and told him to close the bag. The rest of us were waved through without further ado.

However, I digress and to return to our journey there was an uneventful flight to America where Sidney and I as devout Traditional Jazz-men – Sidney a beautiful and accomplished pianist and me very much a hack cornet and trombonist – went 'way down yonder to New Orleans' and spent a day and a night tramping around Beale Street, Canal Street, South Rampart Street, Basin Street and the clubs of the French Quarter. Terrific.

Then on to stay a couple of days in Beverly Hills, Los Angeles, where Sidney, a surgeon, was to lecture at the Cedars of Lebanon Hospital, the famous film star retreat where his friend Craig Heringmann was the chief surgeon. We stayed at the Heringmanns' residence, a visit which sparked a couple of memories which are worth the retelling. Our hosts held a party in our honour and created a truly magnificent buffet meal, the centrepiece being a huge display of prawns in various guises. The hosts were Jewish and you would have laid bets that all the other guests – except me – were of the same faith. I took one look at the prawns, rubbed my hands and thought 'I'm in here!' The locals, however, must have done a deal with the Rabbi as I was practically trampled underfoot when the whistle went and as probably the only Christian all I got were the shells from the prawns.

Whilst Sidney was doing his lecturing bit, I spent most of my time looking out for Doris Day, who apparently walked her dog in the area. No luck there, but I did get an introduction to Nancy Sinatra over the next door garden wall.

Mrs. Heringmann had a maid who at that time could have been described as the epitome of the the Hollywood negro servant image. In today's world I suppose that would be 'Afro-American ladies companion'. Anyway, she was a lovely lady who owned a big car – far bigger than Sidney or I could afford to run – and had a nephew who was the apple of her eye. The relevance of this is explained by the lady washing a couple of my shirts, which were M&S drip dry turquoise blue affairs. Strangely enough, they didn't seem to know about drip dry at that time in California – I expect in Beverly Hills they just chucked their dirty shirts away. She asked me if I would send her nephew a couple on my return to the UK and offered the dollars, but being a decent soul – and overcoming that Yorkshire financial attitude I mentioned earlier – I refused and, on my return, sent a light blue and a white one with my compliments.

Oddly enough, that turquoise shirt came in for another comment when a few days later an airstewardess on an internal Ansett Airlines flight in Australia (not I hasten to add a Qantas flight, known in the trade, so I was told, as 'Quaintarse' because their cabin staff were men, Ducky) said to me "Excuse me, Sir, you have matching shirt and eyes". How's that for an original line? 600 miles an hour and at thirty-odd thousand feet. In all my years of flying that was the nearest I ever came to membership of the Six Mile High Club.

We flew overnight from Los Angeles with a daytime stopover in Hawaii and took an afternoon cruise around Pearl Harbor. Sidney enjoyed the visit and to someone like me who has always been a serious military, naval and aviation buff the experience was truly wonderful. Poignant, but wonderful.

Then we flew on overnight to Australia, calling at Fiji to refuel. If anybody ever asks me if I've been to Fiji I can reply "Yes, but only for a pee". Prior to landing in Australia, breakfast was served and on arrival at Kingsford Smith Airport, Sydney, Walter Griffiths, John Humphreys and Brian LeFevre the Secretary of the Australian Soccer Federation met us and took us to another breakfast. We booked in at the hotel and, as it was the appropriate time and the players were sitting down, I joined them for – breakfast.

What to you may seem like sheer gluttony was in fact perfect preparation for the onslaught that was to follow. At the risk of boring you, I think this insight is worth telling as you will get the feel of things as they happened to us. Breakfast finished and, as the bar was open, I was led there and introduced to several members of the Australian soccer hierarchy. Obviously this meant drinks were served and this is where the triple breakfast paid off. John and Walter had been subjected to a similar welcome in Perth and retired gracefully, knowing what was in store. Sidney was no drinker, so he wasn't much help, so I had to face the Australian openers single-handed. I have never been a spirit drinker and have always stuck to beer and, as some of you no doubt will appreciate, to a man weaned on Wilson's of Manchester and Robinson's of Stockport ales, the local Fosters and Castlemaine held no terrors, although they were considered to be lethal by the natives.

Brian LeFevre, who was a very likeable man and a great help during our tour, actually originated from Wythenshawe in South Manchester and obviously had a great rapport with our party. Quietly, he tipped me off that our hosts' procedure was to get a few drinks down then replace their officials with a fresh lot about every hour on the hour until the visiting person or persons fell over, were sick or died. The idea was that they would put you into a feeling of deep inferiority at the start of what was a very important visit in their ambitions of furthering soccer popularity in their country.

If I never do another thing for England, Harry and St. George, I graduated with honours that day. By lunchtime the last of the deluded buggers staggered away, I went to lunch and then to a darkened room to prepare for the evening's onslaught, which I had been promised would turn the morning's entertainment into pale insignificance.

Actually the dinner with the President and other officials, none of whom had attended the morning's 'Test Match', turned out to be quite a tame affair by comparison. I took it easy and had several substitutes on the team sheet should things turn difficult. Maybe our fame had spread as nobody tried it on our party again during the remainder of the tour.

There were numerous trips overseas with City, each with their own memories, high spots and occasional low points, like sitting for about six hours in the heat at Lagos airport waiting for an aeroplane of which nobody had any knowledge or even cared.

I believe the Australian trip is a good example to illustrate what went on behind the scenes, which after all is why I decided to tell this tale of professional football from the inside. It was interesting and very important that we played our part in promoting 'Soccer' in Australia, which at that time was the up and coming sport Down Under. There had been a large influx of European settlers or immigrants during the '50s and '60s, televised football was being transmitted around the World and we were told that many Australian parents were fed up with their young children getting broken noses and other long term disfigurements or injuries by taking part in rugby or Australian Rules football, which we witnessed to be a mixture of football, rugby and all-in wrestling. It was fascinating to watch football being played on famous grounds such as Brisbane, Adelaide and Melbourne, which are world-renowned as being to cricket what Wembley and St. Andrews are to football and golf.

A most impressive sight met us at Brisbane where hundreds of local youngsters, dressed in their club strips, sat together as teams to watch our match against the local professionals. I suppose that kind of sight no longer is unusual, with thousands of supporters watching their teams whilst wearing replica shirts at about fifty quid a time, but thirty something years ago it was a most memorable and quite moving sight. I think it brought home to us all the reason for playing the games out there and our responsibility for promoting the good things that sport provides in life no matter what the national, social or ethnical background.

Mention of social status reminds me of the surprise it caused when the Australian authorities discovered it was our normal practice for all the party – players and officials – to stay together in the same hotel. Apparently all previous touring sides, which I seem to remember included Manchester United and Arsenal, insisted that their Directors resided in a different establishment from the players and staff. To the very Socialist Australians our togetherness and lack of any class consciousness was quite an eye-opener, very well received and commented upon several occasions. Greece was among other countries where this arrangement caused the same reaction.

All this reminds me that when we arrived at the hotel in Brisbane, of all things that could coincide with the arrival of some twenty odd young, and one or two not so young, fit, heterosexual sportsmen, what should be taking place in the hotel but a Hairdressers Convention and Exhibition. Strewth, Cobber. About one hundred hairdressers and their models, male and female, could have been a recipe for a classic disaster, but to the best of my knowledge nothing untoward took place. With the tonsorial elegance of many of today's players, some of them could be taken for models rather than professional sportsmen – and a few of them ponce about as though they are on the catwalk rather than the pitch.

John and I had an interesting evening out with the cricketing legends, the Chappell brothers, and another of John's friends took John, Sidney, Walter and myself fishing off the Barrier Reef. This was memorable for the photographs I took and threatened to publish in the City programme if ever Walter or John upset me. Despite Walter serving in Royal Navy destroyers during the war, both he and John were badly affected by the swell on the sea, turned a delicate shade of green and took no further part in the day's proceedings. At lunchtime Sidney and I had to go to the other side of the wheelhouse to eat our sandwiches, two lots each.

All this may sound as though tours were merely holidays, which to a certain degree they were, but there was a considerable amount of travel on most trips. Eastern Europe was a difficult place to visit then from food, travel and accommodation angles, although the football people were the same as the World over. They would want to beat you in the game on the day, but then would be good friends, great hosts and fabulous company. We were delighted to be told that we had done a great job in Oz.

IF YOU never travelled in Eastern Europe whilst the 'Iron Curtain' was firmly drawn, don't feel deprived, you didn't miss very much. Obviously I found some parts interesting, but in general the atmosphere and sights were somewhat depressing. For instance in Hungary, whilst staying in Budapest where City were playing Honved, it was plain that all the buildings and houses of that historic city needed a good coat or two of paint. The place gave the general impression of being run down and worn out. We were told by our local contacts that the Communist regime, controlled by Moscow, adopted some sort of deliberate depression policy to keep the people inhibited and from what we could see it appeared to work. Even at the match just about all the spectators, and they were real fans, wore black or dark blue clothing (strange considering the club's red, white and black colours) which gave off a rather dismal and for us a most unusual impression. However, the people themselves were great and organised for our transport the old motor coach used by the famous Hungarian team of the Fifties, complete with wooden seats and built in draughts – in the middle of winter. All we needed was Old Albert to drive it and we would have felt really at home.

I doubt anybody will disagree with me when I say that the Hungarian team of the 1950s probably caused the biggest, most sensational and most deep-seated change of style and attitude in the history of football. Rules have caused changes of style and so on, but Puskas, Hidegkuti and their mates really made the World sit up and take notice with the way their team played the game. People say you always remember where you were when war broke out or when President Kennedy was shot, but I vividly recall watching England being thrashed at Wembley for the first time ever by a foreign team. I was doing my recruit training, square bashing, at RAF West Kirby on the Wirral Peninsular and that particular Wednesday was a day on fatigues duty, my share being sweeping, cleaning and polishing the Sergeants' Mess, or dining and drinking quarters for those of you too young to have enjoyed the highs and lows of National Service. The Mess had a television set, quite a rarity in those days, in fact my Mum and Dad had first got a set in time for the Stanley Matthews Cup final earlier that year, 1953. Fortunately for me several of the sergeants knew that I trained with the Station team and was on City's books, so even as a recruit, the lowest of the low, I was invited (or perhaps it was ordered?) to down mop and duster and join those who were sciving time off to watch the highly publicised game.

History records that we were on the receiving end of an object lesson in how to play the game to the tune of 6-3 and football was never the same again. The so-called deep-lying centre-forward style became world famous and was copied and developed very successfully by Manchester City and perhaps to a lesser extent by West Bromwich Albion.

We ventured behind the Iron Curtain again in the March of 1971 when we flew to Krakow in Poland, some seventy odd miles from Katowice where City were to stay ahead of playing our old adversaries Gornik in the quarter-final European Cup Winners' Cup. We had defeated Gornik in the final the previous season, but now had to cope with home and away legs against them, beginning with this daunting trip. To travel by road in that part of the World at that time of the year was something of a shock, for whilst Poland can be extremely hot in the summer, I soon realised that we were heading towards Siberia in the winter. Snow piled up at the roadsides and the temperature was around minus 15 degrees, which reminded me of the old Air Force ditty about 'cold as a frog in an ice bound pool, cold as the tip of an Eskimo's etc.'. To say it was our first taste of Eastern Europe under the Russian system would be something of an inexactitude, as, thanks to the advice of the British authorities based in Poland, we had brought all our own food and water with us. Sounds a touch dramatic, but we'd heard some tales of food poisoning and suchlike and were not taking any chances.

Another tip off from the Embassy came as I was having a drink in the hotel bar on the day we arrived. The diplomat who had travelled down from Warsaw to make sure we had no problems, and to get tickets for the match, took me to one side and politely suggested I tipped off our party that there was an incurable strain of venereal disease prevalent in that part of the country, a legacy from the Second World War. Obviously I thanked him, adding that we were there to take part in a football match not a sexual contest, although whilst I could speak for the footballers I was not in a position to answer or the Press, who had their own rules. I asked Francis Lee to pass the word around and as far as I know we didn't import anything illegal back into the UK on our return, although one of the media men, sharing a room with a colleague, returned to find the door locked and after knocking had the door opened for him by a young woman wearing his dressing gown. It was probably too cold for such ladies to hang around the streets, but the hotel had an old lady seated at a table at the end of the corridor on each floor who seemed to be the facilitator and timekeeper, change provider and chemist. Had there been any ladies in our party I dread to think what they would have made of the situation and I was doubly glad that we had brought our own food and drink with us.

It was exceptionally cold and Dad, Harry and I bought ourselves fur caps with earmuffs to wear at the match, held at Chorzow. We were very glad to have done so because probably it was the coldest, and noisiest match in my career. The earmuffs kept out the icy wind, but not the noise created by the huge crowd, which was indescribable and the result of virtually all the one hundred thousand supporters blowing bugles or hooters, banging drums and shouting non stop throughout the game. The pitch had been cleared of snow, but was rock hard and, despite having some special studs fitted to our players boots, the Polish lads generally coped far better with the conditions and the great inside forward Lubanski was outstanding. It's always a joy to watch a great player at the peak of his powers, even if he is taking your own team apart. City did well enough considering the conditions and held Gornik to a respectable 0-2 result, giving us a chance in the return leg.

Next morning we were on the coach, ready to set off for the airport only to discover we were waiting for the same gentleman of the Press who'd had the guest in his room. He eventually appeared and Dad, I'm sure totally unaware of what had been going on, said, "Here he is, give him a clap". I commented to Harry and Walter that I hoped the journalist hadn't contracted the incurable kind the previous night.

As usual we had travelled by chartered BEA Comet, the crew staying with us and attending the match, but on arrival at Krakow Airport the pilots found fairly thick mist enveloping the area and snow lying about both on and off the runway. The authorities were not very cooperative and whilst the crew were attempting to get permission to take off, the rest of the party tried to spend our Polish zloti, which the rules stated could not be taken out of the country. Some had drinks or bought bottles of vodka, but Polish pork products have always been famous and I bought a few tins of ham and some Polish farmer's ring. No snide giggles, please, the farmer's ring is a spiced sausage which is an excellent meal when complemented by sauerkraut. Eventually we boarded the Comet and the pilot cautiously taxied along the runway and back again in the misty and, under normal conditions, unacceptable visibility. The Captain came back into the cabin and spoke to Walter, Dad and I, saying he was going to take off there and then as he was not impressed with the so-called cooperation from the authorities and the forecast was getting worse. The much-maligned de Havilland Comet was a magnificent aeroplane with a huge reserve of power and as our load was nowhere near capacity we took off like a fighter plane. A reserve engineer sitting across the aisle from me laughed and said it was the shortest take off he could remember. Later in the flight, when it wouldn't cause any heart failures, the Captain came over the Tannoy system and said he had taxied up and down the runway and got up fast as he did not feel comfortable about possible vehicles and so on which might 'accidentally', shall we say, have been left adjacent to the mist shrouded runway. All's well that ends well, but we learned that our supporters, who travelled separately on an aircraft chartered from another company, were stranded for two more days.

Whilst in Katowice, Dad, Walter Griffiths, Harry and I visited the Auschwitz/Birkenau concentration camp, the site of probably the Second World War's worst atrocities. Peter Gardner from the *Manchester Evening News* had been before in 1966 when England had played a World Cup warm up game nearby. The other newspaper lads did not want to come with us or had something else to do (particularly in one case) and we would not allow the players to possibly become unsettled by the rather gruesome experience. Harry and I, in particular, knew a considerable amount of detail because of our mutual and avid interest in history and wars. Dad had been gassed by the Germans in the First World War and Walter had served in the Royal Navy in the Second, so you might say that we were not quite your average visitors of thirty odd years ago. No doubt it is a sombre place at the best of times, it certainly was that day, with a touch of snow in the air and virtually nobody else around the surprisingly large site.

We walked into the gas chambers, saw the ovens in which the bodies were cremated, viewed the piles of artificial limbs, children's toys and other disgusting sights but the most gratifying was the special gallows which had been built to hang the former camp Commandant, Rudolf Hoess, as a war criminal in 1947. I remember saying to Harry it would have been fitting if all those looking down from Heaven, or those looking up from Hell, had witnessed that event. Even to a person such as myself who is blessed with a rather unemotional nature that experience was quite something.

The return match was won 2-0 by City, which, as penalty shoot-outs had not yet been introduced, meant a replay in neutral Copenhagen and on this occasion the usual administrative team of Walter Griffiths, Dad and myself, together with

Harry Finlaison, who at John Humphreys' suggestion was to be co-opted onto the Board at the end of the season, was supplemented by John's brother Stuart Humphreys and several others. One of these was John Griffith, a First Division referee, who being local to Manchester obviously could never take any of City or United's games, but who enjoyed acting as host and coordinator for the club for visiting overseas referees. Harry's business was Danish-based textile machinery and he knew Copenhagen like the back of his hand. Not only did he, Walter and I get a liquid tour and lunch at the Tuborg factory, but we were invited to some club or another where the evening finished up with all the guests standing (those who still could, at least) with one foot on the bench seats, the other foot on the tables and drinking toasts to friendship or whatever. Funny how you usually only remember the unfortunate incidents that happen to other people, but I suppose that is what makes them funny. On this occasion Griffith missed the table with his foot, slipped underneath, in the process bashing his nose, which squirted blood all over the place, in particular covering Stewart Humphreys' shirt. His own was well-doused in claret and the incident reminded me that the one serious conviction a man should have is that nothing should be taken too seriously.

Next day City won the replay 3-1 and the idea of toasts to friendship and the like came into perspective somewhat when the President of Gornik complained to the football authorities that the City players had been on drugs both in Poland and the return match. The players and ourselves naturally were indignant and disgusted by the insinuation, but the authorities had no option but to carry out tests. A draw was made for the random selection of three players, who were, I believe, Derek Jeffries, Colin Bell and David Connor. The three all struggled hard to provide samples even after being filled up with orange juice. Naturally the tests were negative and after the rather snide attempt to put the players off, it was an extra satisfaction to win the tie and progress to the semi-final, which, with a much-depleted side, we lost over two legs to eventual winners Chelsea.

That was not the only aeroplane incident City have suffered. In 2006 the Directors and Secretary were returning from a match at Portsmouth when their chartered aeroplane developed serious problems shortly after take off, as one of the two engines malfunctioned and cut out. Fortunately the pilot had sufficient height, allowing him to force land at nearby Farnborough airfield and the incident ended up without any injuries and with understandable relief all round. Visions of

Torino FC, the Zambian national team and, in particular for me, Manchester United come vividly to mind at such times and I think if most people are honest they put up with flying as a means to an end, and are relieved when safely back on the ground. Footballers are no exception and I remember City full-back of the early 1970s Arthur Mann had to be carried off an aeroplane and sedated on one occasion as we readied for take off on the return trip from one of our European ties. As hard-working and dependable a player as you could come across, Alan Oakes hated flying and broke as much sweat waiting to board a flight as he did during ninety minutes on a Saturday afternoon, that being the time football was usually played in those days. One time we had to wait a few hours at Manchester Airport whilst an engine was changed and poor old Alan's nerves really suffered.

It was a bit different for me. With the family flying connections I mentioned earlier, I had been introduced to flying, and its perils, at an early age and have got some 71 years and a thousand or two hours as a passenger, and some pilot experience, under my belt in private, commercial and military aeroplanes, from biplanes to jumbo jets. Up to now I have been very fortunate, with only a handful of unpalatable moments to mar all the good memories. A hairy descent into Barcelona, shared by Alan Oakes, practising emergency landings during pilot training and once being hit by lightning approaching Manchester.

Fingers crossed, lads.

Such experiences are not in the least bit funny at the time, but they must surely be the finest cure for constipation known to man.

MOST CERTAINLY I did not invent the wheel, but I had several original ideas, some of which have been successful, some would have been with backing and some have worked for others who had visionary colleagues. I should like to spend a little time talking about a few of those ideas which I hope will be of interest to you and perhaps provide a background to some things which in today's world are taken for granted.

During the 1970s I talked with Alan Hardaker, Secretary of the Football League, and George Readle, his deputy, about sponsorship in football. Alan was a tough operator – could turn and twist some of the old fogies who ran the Football League round his little finger and most Directors went in fear and dread of him. George, a former referee, was a kindly and cheerful man. I seemed to get on alright with Alan because we both called a spade a spade and, when required, a bloody shovel. As a former Town Clerk in Yorkshire he would not tolerate fools, but if he thought you knew what you were talking about you were OK. My professional background as an industrial artist and designer was linked to advertising and public relations and I had looked closely at sponsored advertising, something which simply did not exist in the game thirty-five years ago. With a small amount of support from some members of the League Management Committee, I approached the Ford Motor Company with an offer which I felt could bear fruit. There is no point in publishing my correspondence to Ford, but the reply from their Advertising and Sales Promotion Manager makes interesting reading in the light of how sponsorship has subsequently developed, especially bearing in mind the company's long-standing sponsorship of Sky TV's Premier League coverage.

My proposals were sold to them as 'total sponsorship and its obvious spinoffs, of the Football League First, Second, Third and Fourth divisions, which will be known as the 'FORD ENGLISH LEAGUE' or 'FORD FIRST DIVISION' or similar for the sum of one million pounds.' Some nerve in those days, eh?

The sponsorship of the Football League Cup was proposed, with similar amendments to the title, and I added a further idea which was a touch cheeky but at the same time eventually turned out to be a real moneymaker all round.

'The Ford name and logo could feature on the front of Manchester City FC shirts and literature for a fee of £50,000 per season.' How about that, then?

Those were my words many years ago. Little did Ford, or myself for that matter, realise what would come to pass in the not too distant future and you only have to look at your television set to see the Ford logo on shirts all over the World, including rugby players as far away as Australia.

The reply I received is reprinted here in full.

Ford Motor Company Limited
Central Office
Eagle Way
Brentford
Essex CM13 3BW
Mr A E Alexander MSIAD MAIDO

Dear Mr Alexander

Thank you for your letter of April 10 regarding our possible sponsorship of the English Football League.

Your proposals are certainly novel and ambitious, and as such we have given them very careful consideration. Regrettably, however, I must confirm to you that we have decided to maintain our policy of devoting our advertising and sales promotion funds to activities which have more direct exposure of our products than is implicit in the kind of sponsorship you are offering. Ours is one of the world's best-known trade-names and we therefore generally seek to promote the benefits of owning and operating a Ford vehicle in preference to promoting the name 'Ford' in isolation.

The same marketing philosophy applies to your additional suggestion regarding shirt advertising for Manchester City Football Club. It may however, be more appropriate for one of the Ford Main Dealers in the Greater Manchester area to adopt this form of advertising, and I would therefore suggest you contact them directly.

Thank you for offering us the opportunity of sponsorship and I regret that on this occasion we cannot progress your proposal further.

Yours sincerely,

I M Seear
Manager, Car Advertising & Sales Promotion

Your fans and your team were the considerations when I became a Director, and certainly at City we tried to improve the facilities for the supporters, who any responsible person realised were the lifeblood of the club and the very reason for its existence. In 1968 plans were afoot to rebuild the North Stand at Maine Road and with the financial rewards of the success of recent seasons available it was decided to go ahead with redeveloping the structure, which had originated in 1923 as the Scoreboard End and had been part of the stadium that housed the English record crowd outside Wembley of 84,000 plus when Stoke City, and their mercurial winger Stanley Matthews visited in March 1934 for an FA Cup quarter-final.

Another big concern was to use up profits made during any financial year and thus avoid paying tax to the Government and so allow the money 'go out of football'. Before a politician or two starts to jump out of their prams, I don't suppose for one minute that it cost any Government very much in revenue because it was a minor miracle in those days if anybody made a profit. Many small clubs relied on the generosity of their Chairman and Directors for their continued existence and, when talking football, that should never be forgotten in these days of multi-million pound annual salaries and similarly grotesque commercial deals. Professional football is not just about half a dozen clubs owned, or desired to be owned, by people from all over the World.

So, hence the new North Stand. A company called the Cheshire Design Group was asked to provide ideas for the proposed development and I was asked, due to my professional background, along with Secretary Walter Griffiths to liaise with the architects and the Board. The chief partner of Cheshire Design Group, Harry Marsland, and I saw eye to eye on most things and eventually spent some time 'pipe dreaming' about stadia and possible facilities for the future.

A fair amount of original ideas were examined, one of the best being Drive In Soccer, where the old Kippax Stand facing the Main Stand could be rebuilt. City were fortunate, or farsighted, in as much as a considerable amount of land around the ground was owned by the Club and could be developed. The idea we came up with was to construct a new stand with integral car parking and dining, or hospitality, suites which clients (the posh name for supporters who would pay a bit more) could access directly from their cars or taxis without being exposed to the elements. They could then eat, drink and be merry with their friends or customers and could watch the match in comfort from either open air or from behind sliding glass windows/doors.

Nobody else had anything remotely like that at the time and I still have the drawings and plans for the project, which probably would have gone ahead in the early seventies had not the club by then have been in the overall control of the Smith/Swales consortium (of which more later), who were against spending money on anything unless it was broken, in their own interests or a transfer whim of Malcolm Allison.

THE HEAD groundsman at Maine Road from 1960 to 1997 was Stan Gibson, whose house, situated between the Stadium, the Social Club and the Club Superstore, meant that he literally lived on the job. It was more than just a job to Stan and he was always receptive to new ideas even when we found they would be impractical. My golfing background provided the knowledge and detail for the selective watering system about which he enthused when I suggested it could work for a football pitch and save time and trouble.

Stan started working with me in 1968, when I became the Director responsible for the Maine Road and training pitches, and because we shared a knowledge of turf, and the belief that you can't mess about with nature, we got along together like the proverbial house on fire.

We held strong views that it is no use having good players if you do not have a first class pitch for them to play on, a problem that has been obvious at some other well-known clubs in more recent times. The soil and sub-soil of the Maine Road pitch had become compacted over many years and water could not be drained away quickly or satisfactorily, so the following close season the playing pitch was dug up, the soil broken down and special sand mixed with it. The area was then re-seeded rather than re-turfed, as that can cause serious problems. During that summer Stan and I kept our fingers crossed as he nurtured the pitch like a new baby.

It was all worthwhile when we finished up with a playing surface which many referees and players reckoned was second to none in the League. A year or so later City became the first club to have an automatic water sprinkler and irrigation system, controlled from a switchboard in the Groundsman's room in the main stand. This meant Stan could water the pitch whilst sitting with his feet up and a cup of tea in his hand. It was a very complex system which could be tuned to suit particular players. Tony Book liked his parts of the pitch to be fairly firm, so those bits didn't get much water before a game.

Stan and I had the odd spot of trouble with Malcolm Allison when he trained the players on the pitch instead of the training ground, but it was usually resolved with a war of words rather than physical violence. We accommodated the various whims of the managerial hierarchy, for example when it was decided to concentrate on playing wingers, we had the pitch widened to give them more room and allow, theoretically, City to gain an advantage. Other clubs, for example Liverpool, had small pitches and it was felt that gave them an advantage when playing at home. Generally this was due to the restrictions of the club's ground area and City were lucky to have a pitch that could be maximum size and as big as Wembley.

We became the first club to operate a really satisfactory system for keeping the pitch clear of frost and snow, giving Stan the chance to take pride that City could put on games when most of the country had unplayable grounds. That happened after I was approached by a Swedish company, through their British agents, regarding a system which was being used extensively throughout Sweden to keep hospital car parks and similar places clear of ice and freezing up. The clever idea was to use waste steam and other generated heat that otherwise would simply be dissipated in the atmosphere. This wasted heat was piped under the surface of the car park or wherever and kept the ground temperature just above freezing level.

I was very impressed with the details supplied to me and, despite the scepticism of the other Directors, was taken out to Sweden by the company and shown round several sites using the system in different ways. As a quick aside, I was invited to all sorts of Swedish Nights Out for Tired Businessmen, but thought that I had better behave myself as we were potential buyers. I got to bed at a reasonable time and awoke in blazing sunshine, leapt out of bed and into the bathroom, shaved and washed and went back into the bedroom to discover it was actually five minutes past three in the morning. I had forgotten the Midnight Sun that applies in northern parts at that time of the year.

The upshot was that we had the system installed for a cost of some £40,000. Then Chairman Peter Swales was horrified, but the financial recuperation soon brought a few smiles to previously doubtful faces. As the club did not generate anything like enough waste steam in the course of normal activities, we bought a gas boiler to create the necessary heat for the undersoil piping. The big difference to all the other systems around the country at that time was that we prevented frost and ice forming by keeping the ground at a temperature slightly above freezing point, as opposed to all the others which simply melted the snow, ice or whatever and left puddles, creating waterlogging and mud. Stan and I kept in touch with the weather forecasting unit at Manchester Airport and the radio stations, switching the boiler on about

Thursday if the forecast was the least bit dodgy. The gentle heat as opposed to the flame-thrower type technique did not damage the turf and in fact extended the growing season by some useful time at both ends of the season.

The financial advantage was that when most other matches were called off for unplayable pitches, the football public and the television companies knew City would be playing and featured our game, bringing in some useful revenue. Also it meant that we would sell all our programmes which was quite a wasted cost if your match was called off.

I think one or two of the Directors who previously thought I knew nowt about financial matters treated me with a bit more respect after the first game or two, particularly as I was trundled around England and Scotland advising other clubs following our success and the considerable publicity. Everton were one such club and during the season prior to renovating the pitch at Goodison Park, I went on to their playing area before our Cup match with them and could smell the stale and sour earth. The following Wednesday, before the replay, I was on the Maine Road pitch chatting with the referee, Peter Willis. We had both noticed the smell and condition of the Goodison pitch the previous Saturday. Jim Greenwood was the Everton secretary at that time. He and I were friendly and we talked about pitch problems and cures. His club carried out considerable remedial work and installed undersoil heating shortly afterwards and produced a superb playing area.

Stan Gibson and I always had great respect for each other, were good workmates and friends, enjoying an occasional Guinness after a job well done. As Stan died a couple of years ago I would like to take this opportunity to thank his family for his friendship and the quality of his work.

THIRTY-FIVE YEARS ago it was reported that:

'Manchester City are to have one of the biggest and best-equipped Soccer training camps in Europe. They are in the final stage of negotiations for an attractive, rural, twelve acre site off Manchester Road, Cheadle. And when the big £70,000 operation of converting it into a modern training establishment is completed, their players will see Maine Road only on match days.

There will be two pitches – one of them with soil heating equipment – a running track, a gymnasium, dressing and treatment rooms, and a canteen for the staff and players. In addition to a sauna bath, there will be remedial baths of the type which City's players now have to travel to Blackpool to use.

Director Eric Alexander, who heads the stadium and training sub committee, confirmed last night that plans had been prepared and the project was almost underway.   He said Joe Mercer and Malcolm Allison are very enthusiastic about it. "We have made a long search for a site and this looks like the ideal one. It is pleasantly landscaped and it will give the playing staff a wonderful environment for training away from the atmosphere of Maine Road".

Manager Joe Mercer said last night, "It will take the players away from the pressures which they can come under at the ground, and it will keep the Maine Road pitch free from non-match days." City, whose new £360,000 North Stand will open for the start of the season regard the training camp training project as one of their most exciting developments.'

Of City's detailed plans I explained that we had done an enormous amount of research and wherever we had been in Europe we inspected other clubs facilities and asked them about any snags. Over a long period we had built up a dossier of the best features to embrace in the scheme. We were determined to profit by any mistakes other clubs admitted to making.

Sadly, this project was to become another victim of the Johnson sell out to Smith, Cussons and Co.

'The Bible tells us to love our neighbours, also our enemies, probably because they are generally the same people.'
GK Chesterton

Incidentally a friend of mine, Trevor, had to go into hospital recently and I visited him in the Alexandra Hospital (no relation) in Cheadle, which is adjacent to the site of those 'state of the art' training facilities that was intended to be constructed all those years ago. The area is now a cemetery, something which struck me a rather apt.

I was fed up about it at the time, but as I write this the more I realise what a shambles that lot made of the club (more of which later), one from which despite the honest efforts of several decent men and countless millions of pounds it still has not truly recovered. Had we been able to carry on with that and other innovations, who knows to what it may have led, not only for City but football and sport in general. If sponsorship had been accepted who knows what else may have followed?

Another interesting insight to the big business world came my way when I sat in on an interview between City director Robert Harris and a representative of some firm or another who wanted to sell City a product. At that time Harris was the Chairman of Great Universal Stores, the mail order giants with numerous catalogues to their name, and listening to him bargaining was quite revelation to a country boy like me. Robert's final killer punch was "Well Mr X we would really like to do business with you and your company, but unfortunately your price is just outside our budget. If however you could come down, say two pence per item we could take another look at it". I really felt for the guy who I'm certain had already gone lower than he was permitted in the hope of getting Manchester City in his order book.

Agents would have received short shift in those days, as money was hard to come by and directors did not mortgage their clubs for the next fifty years on the whim of the Chairman or some domineering Manager.

For me an amusing and I'm sure unusual situation existed between Harris and myself. I had a short contract with a Manchester based advertising company, generally employed to use my contacts rather than my professional skills as an industrial designer and commercial artist and one of the very important accounts to the agency was the aforementioned Great Universal Stores where Robert Harris sat on his golden throne.

So, we had the silly situation where on Mondays, Wednesdays unless there was a match, Thursdays and Fridays it was Mr. Harris, Chairman, Sir, from me and on Tuesdays, City board meeting night, and Saturdays it was Mr A, Eric or Mr. Chairman from him.

Another incident around that time demonstrating what a democracy football used to be not that many years ago, was several days after attending a big FA or Football League meeting for Chairmen in London, I was walking down the Agency exit corridor on my way home when I met a party of people entering the building. One was the Managing Director of the Company, whom I'm sure did not really approve of my appointment as he did not have much interest in sport and I think was originally an architect by profession and in my time architects and 'real' artists were like Christians and lions. Anyway, among this party obviously being feted by the hierarchy was the Chairman of a minor and recently elected League club and who had sat in my company at the football meeting, become friendly and pleased to be in the company of the Chairman of one of the top clubs. He spotted me "Good Heavens, Mr. Alexander (Mr. Alexander, mark you) what are you doing here?"

"Actually I work for this company, Fred or Charlie (or whatever his name was and I'm sorry I can't recall it but it was over thirty years ago)."

This chap was the Chairman of what certainly at that time was one of if not the biggest media set ups in Britain and a very, very important gentleman in that area.

"You are very lucky having someone like Eric working with you. He will be joining us for dinner, won't he?"

Oh boy, I could not have written the script, the M.D. nearly died on the spot, spluttered an invitation to join the party at the Midland Hotel French Restaurant, which I accepted with due grace, and the gentleman in question spent the next few hours discussing football with me. I don't know what the business outcome was from the evening, but I recall that in the best French restaurant in Manchester they served salt in mistake for sugar with the strawberries and cream. As a non sugar user that gave me another quiet giggle at the MD's expense and after that I decided that I was probably too irreverent to work for other people and only worked for myself from then onwards.

There is nothing clever in it, but having been born with an ear and something of a flair for accents and languages, including bad, I have always quite enjoyed telling jokes and stories with an accent or dialect. My friend Harry Glen Finlaison, despite his Scottish ancestry, was literally born on the banks of the Thames and after more than fifty years of friendship we still rib each other over our North versus South pronunciations. We both saw the film 'Tunes of Glory' about forty years ago and occasionally make comments to each other in a satirical mimicry of Alec Guinness's Scottish colonel voice 'Aye Laddie, he's no due till the morn' and so on. Probably a bit childish by some people's standards, but we still have a laugh. The point being that Ron Crowther of the *Daily Mail*, a very conscientious football and sports journalist, after he had completed any work schedule often gave vent to his rather quiet sense of humour and was a very good mimic of several well known personalities. Without being disrespectful, a quite remarkable achievement in the profession, he could do a hilarious take off of United's Chairman, Louis Edwards, and sometimes when we were abroad he and I would hold a United Board Meeting. Ron took Louis and Alan Gibson, son of the famous former Chairman and who was a really nice man with a distinctive shy manner, and I did Matt Busby and Denzel Haroun. All good clean fun. We had played in Norway and in the bar after the game Ron had us all in stitches laughing at his impersonation of City's director Michael Horwich, another person with a somewhat unique voice and delivery. The next day we travelled to Holland and Michael joined up with us for whatever match was to complete the tour. He has a good sense of humour, sometimes you needed one to be a City director, and when we told him of the previous night's hilarity he insisted Ron repeated his act and Micheal to his credit joined in. He tends to splash a bit when excited and the rest of us had to take cover with two of them at it.

Maybe this helps to prove that although perhaps not perfect gentlemen some of we directors do not and did not spend our overseas time in seedy night clubs and getting our names in the papers for all the wrong reasons.

Boys will be boys, unfortunately so will some middle-aged men.

I WAS reminded of the following incident the other day when I was taking one of my occasional rides into Douglas on the Isle of Man Victorian Steam Railway, a superbly maintained attraction you should try if you are ever in this neck of the woods. Railways were our recognised mode of travel to the Big City in the Sixties and Seventies, before Chairmen with private jets.

On this particular occasion City beat United in a midweek Cup game, and there was to be a Football League Chairmen's meeting in London the next day, so after the game United Chairman, Louis Edwards, Sir Matt Busby and myself arranged to travel together on the morning train. Matt boarded in Manchester and Louis and myself joined him at Wilmslow station. As the train pulled in Matt's head popped out of a window to direct us to the seats he had saved us in the breakfast compartment. When we sat down together the steward made a surprised comment about us being friends and travelling together, particularly after the previous night's result.

We had a great journey down with plenty of interesting conversation, including Louis regaling Matt and I with some of his exploits on the Stock Market. Being on the Management Committee he was to attend the Committee lunch whilst Matt and I were to go to the main meeting in the afternoon. We had to find a way to while away the time and there looked to be a decent pub across the road from our hotel, so I said to Matt that I was not interested in an hotel lunch, but would be going across the road for a pie and a pint. To my surprise he asked if he could come with me, saying that he had not done anything like that for years. We sat down in the pub and were talking about this, that and the other when newspaper reporter Steve Curry came in. He went to the bar, got his drink, turned round and saw us, did a double take and came over to our table. He was totally surprised at Matt and I drinking together and enjoying each other's company, commenting on the previous evening's score and remarking that it was very unusual to see two rivals so friendly. Patiently Matt and I explained that we were lifelong friends and that a few football results were not going to alter anything. When we left the pub, Matt said it was the best lunchtime he had spent in London for a very long time. On returning to the hotel for the meeting we met Doug Ellis, or 'Deadly Doug' as sometimes he was referred to in the Press during his many years (and managers) as Chairman of Aston Villa. At that time Villa had just come up from the Third Division and were attempting to struggle out of the Second and into the First Division. Doug was full of ideas, which he insisted on telling us about, concluding with the words, "When I get back in the First Division, Matt, just watch me go" (note the 'I's and 'Me's with which the conversation was littered).

> *'The personal pronoun 'I' should be the coat-of-arms of some individuals.'*
> de Riverol

As we went through to the meeting Matt nudged me, saying in my ear, "Our Mr. Ellis is going to be a very busy man, eh, Eric"!

In fact when Villa did get back into the First Division, Doug had some success with the Two Ronnies (Saunders and Atkinson that is, not the comedians . . . I don't know though, perhaps that's a matter of opinion?!) He kept going as chairman at Villa until he was over 80 years of age. There is hope for me yet.

I WROTE this piece years ago when we were flying to Italy to play Inter Milan.

The sun was very bright at 29,000 feet over the centre of Europe and the glass of British Airways champagne with lunch had brought on a mellow mood as I looked down at the indescribable beauty and grandeur of the Central Alps. The various shades of brown and grey with very few signs of snow made it a superb sight, and I thought back over twenty years to when I used to spend a month of my summer holidays each year climbing on those very slopes, now seen from a vastly different angle. In those days little did I think that I would hurtle over the peaks of the Mont Blanc massif at some 600 miles per hour in an aluminium tube containing one of the most valuable and expensive cargoes you could imagine. Chamonix railway station came to mind and I recalled that after four weeks in the wilds and not a newspaper in sight (bliss) I saw an English paper and read that City had signed Roy Paul, one of the World Cup defectors to Bogota, who became a magnificent captain and inspiration to City during the 1950's and an integral part of the so-called 'Revie Plan'.

This reminded me of some of the great names at the club during that era and made me think about some of the City players I had seen and in some cases trained with and played alongside. What would the best team be if it were possible to select eleven men from my personal recollections of that period, considering the differing styles of play that have developed over the past twenty years or so.

The names flashed past like the scenery below, Ray Haddington, probably the hardest shot I ever saw, those two stylish wing halves from Ireland, Billy Walsh, who incidentally must hold some sort of record having represented England, Northern Ireland and Eire, and Frank 'Clancy' McCourt, who finished his training each day betting and taking penalties against Bert Trautmann. Those tremendous clubmen who always gave 100% plus, Johnny Hart and Roy Clarke. The wing dazzlers, Ray Sambrook, Bill Spurdle, Billy Linacre and Jackie Oakes of the devastating left foot and who patiently taught me how to nudge a full back when he was on his 'far' leg. The three Erics, Eastwood, Westwood and Williams. The one season goal-scoring machine Alex Harley, who unfortunately did not seem to fit in with the other ten players. Joe Fagan, dominant centre-half and another of Dad's lads, now a tower of strength in the Liverpool set up. Eddie McMorran who headed a goal direct from a Sam Bartram goal kick. Les McDowall, a centre-half, who was rugged yet cultured and graceful before he became a far-sighted manager of the club from 1950 to 1963, probably twenty years ahead of his time.

The many unlucky goalkeepers who could not get a regular first team place because of the 'Big Three' goalkeepers of the past forty or so years, Frank Swift, Bert Trautmann and recently Joe Corrigan, Ken Barnes and Johnny Williamson of the Revie Plan, Don himself and so on . . .

I got to thinking about what my best 'traditional' team would be to play my best team of the then current period – the late seventies – playing in the style of the day. Other people's ideas of teams are never much interest to anybody else so we can leave that bit as the seat belt sign has gone on and we are approaching Milan Airport. Milan. Jimmy Greaves territory. He wasn't a bad player either, although I'm told he didn't exactly enjoy his rather brief sojourn with the Italians.

Incidentally, we were playing in Greece one time and having an evening meal together were Joe Mercer, Malcolm Allison, the former Manchester United, Newcastle and England (and Bogota exile) winger Charlie Mitten, former City centre half and trainer Dave Ewing and the legendary wing half of the Revie Plan, Ken Barnes. All sorts of memories were talked over and eventually, after listening entranced to my elders and betters, I asked what would happen if a team went out with no pre-match notification to the opposition and played the traditional 'W' formation with full-backs, half-backs, inside-forwards and wingers? This provoked some laughter and some serious consideration. The concensus of opinion was the old style team would totally puzzle the modern lads for about twenty minutes but would then be taken apart. Interesting, as quite often you hear older people talking about the 'good old days', and perhaps they were not quite as good as we remember.

Perhaps once again distance lending enchantment . . .

One player who would have stood a chance of getting into my team if he'd ever played for City is George Best. What an abundance of talent the man possessed and I enjoyed getting to know him, as the two clubs shared social activities far more back in the day. In recent times the Isle of Man has become a popular location for films and videos and I have taken part, as an extra, in several productions. One such, "The George Best Story", was filmed in 2000 and featured 'George' and, in places, 'Rodney Marsh', obviously with both of whom I was acquainted in real life. Nobody on set was aware of this, though, and I didn't say anything, but one close up scene showed 'George' and myself playing roulette in a casino. I was tolerating George's alcoholic activities and social altercations, whilst attempting to enjoy the evening, and I wondered at the time if anybody watching the completed film would recognise me and think, 'what a coincidence – George Best drinking, gambling and 'birding' with the Chairman of Manchester City.'

Whenever the real life George hit the headlines with his not so private activities, some people would talk about him in hallowed tones as the greatest footballer of all time or the best British player ever, as an expression of the talent they believed he had wasted. Many, like me, fail to understand how it is possible to compare a forward with, for instance, goalkeepers like Frank Swift and Peter Shilton, full-backs like Jimmy Armfield and Ray Wilson, half-backs like Billy Wright, John Charles and Duncan Edwards (who was still nowhere near the finished article when he was killed). Most of those making such a claim are too young or never saw Stanley Matthews, Tom Finney, Johnny Haynes or Peter Doherty, to name but a few of many greats of the game it's been my pleasure to watch. George was a great player with incredible ball control, balance and vision and his contribution to football should be judged on those counts and not on his off field activities. However there are always tall tales that circulate about so-called legends that tend to be nothing more than myths. Among others I once read was about the time in December 1970 that City beat United 4-1 at Old Trafford and one or two of the United players were getting somewhat frustrated towards the end of the game. City's young full-back Glyn Pardoe had played Best virtually out of the game and eventually suffered horrendous injuries from a tackle by George, an incident which did not endear Best to some of the City players, officials and fans. Pardoe was rushed to hospital with life-threatening injuries and it was decided to amputate his leg in order to save his life. However, a last minute attempt to get the blood flowing was successful and his life and his leg were saved, although the incident virtually finished his career. Glyn had played for England Schoolboys, Young England and the Under 21s, was extremely fit and later told me that he had hoped to play until at least his mid-thirties, having already won Second Division Championship, First Division Championship, FA Cup, Football League Cup and European Cup Winners Cup medals. Pardoe was a fabulously talented footballer who could, and did, play anywhere from full-back to outside left with obvious class. The myth bit I mentioned was that George sent Glyn flowers every day whilst in hospital. Now I know for cast iron certainty that Glyn never had any such flowers and, although Best did eventually visit him, it appeared to be 'under instructions', and, in fact, he expressed no regrets or sympathy.

Glyn Pardoe and his cousin Alan Oakes were two fine examples of dedicated, keen and decent-living sportsmen, who were a credit to football, Manchester City Football Club, themselves and their families. Glyn went on to coach many of City's youngsters through the very successful and rewarding late Seventies and Eighties, while Alan is still the holder of the record number of appearances for City – 669 in 17 years with the club.

FOR MANY years my wife Mavis and I have visited Malta as one of our favourite holiday destinations, following my introduction to the island via a visit with Manchester City for a mid-season break in 1971, I have come to know several of the Maltese football officials quite well. One of them, Michael Tabona, 'Mr. Mike', despite being a rabid Manchester United fan and friend of Matt Busby and Louis Edwards, became a good friend of ours and, as the Managing Director of a fine hotel, it was natural that eventually we went to stay with him and became regular guests.

During one holiday there Mavis and I decided to go on a round the island boat cruise which was run by the hotel, who also own the shipping company. Mavis is not a good sailor and we waited until the day in question before deciding to take up the day cruise, and having seen the sunny and calm weather, arrived at the landing stage just prior to the ship's departure. Mavis looked after the presentation of the tickets and I went on to the top deck of the vessel to try and obtain two seats butting onto the rails and giving an unrestricted view. Having been on the cruise myself on several occasions, I knew which side of the vessel would be facing the Island on its round trip, which was obviously the side to select. There were just two seats which suited the purpose and one of them had a bag with scuba diving equipment on it. I asked the lady and gentleman sitting in the facing seats if the two places were vacant and they instantly said yes and moved the bag onto the floor. I sat down and Mavis joined me a few moments later. During the next hour or so, we spoke on a couple of occasions with the other couple, once when they offered Mavis a towel to sit on to cushion the wooden seat. At lunch time we anchored in a bay where anybody who wanted to swim or scuba dive had an hour to do so whilst the others had a buffet lunch on the ship. The couple opposite had intended diving and we said we would look after their clothes and stuff, but the lady decided to give it a miss and her husband went off on his own. Obviously this led to a conversation starting and she asked us at which hotel we were staying and we told her the Fortina Spa Resort, which surprised her and said they had intended going to the Fortina but the travel agent had recommended a hotel which he thought would suit them better. However they liked going out in the evenings and their hotel was, to use her expression, 'miles from anywhere'. She then asked all about our hotel and how we came to stay there the first time and I told I had got to know Michael Tabona through football on the Island.

There was a pause for several minutes and we watched for her husband to appear in the water along side the ship and then quite out of the blue she asked if I was interested in football, and who did I support. I am always very cagey about disclosing my background, particularly to strangers, and I simply responded by saying, "do you follow football, and where do you come from?" She had no apparent accent that I could recognise and I was very surprised when she said Manchester. Now, traditionally United drew their supporters from the north and west of Manchester and City, certainly in the old days, from the east and south, so I asked which part of Manchester, and she answered the middle, St. Mary's area, which meant nothing to me. There was another pause before what was literally a bolt from the blue when she said, "My great uncle was the Chairman of Manchester City".

Now I've come across that sort of thing before, but this was really creepy and so I simply said, "Oh yes, who was that?"

"Albert Alexander."

We have all heard of the hairs standing up on the back of your neck, but believe me they really did on mine, as well as those on my arms and legs. Mavis said later that she had the same sensation.

"Really, what was your maiden name, then?" I asked.

"Priestnell."

Now it was her turn to get the standing hair treatment. My mother's brother had two sons, one I knew had no family, so I ventured, "You must be Ken's daughter. He's my cousin, although I have not heard anything of him since I was a young man. I'm Eric Alexander, Albert was my father, so we must be second cousins or something."

A deathly white face with a couple of tears running down, she couldn't say anything for a moment or two. Then Heather, as she told us her name was, Mavis and I started a most unusual and fascinating conversation. Without going into inconsequential detail, her father Kenneth had been rather the black sheep of his family, a very fine singer, but with something of an over enthusiasm for alcohol and he had more or less disappeared from our view when I was still a young man, so I knew nothing of any family. Heather knew nothing of my existence or our side of the family and when her father and mother parted when she was a child she lost contact with her other relations.

When her husband Mike returned from his swim we set him up for quite a surprise and he, too, got the shock treatment.

That was the most incredible coincidence that I have ever come across when you consider the chain of events. Both couples making a last minute decision to take the cruise, the only two seats available, Mike going for a swim on his own, as had Heather gone with him as originally intended the critical conversation would never had taken place, the interest in our respective hotels and the obscure reference to the Fortina and the football connections.

HOWEVER, MALTA has not only held happy memories for me. When Joe Mercer came to City in 1965 and employed Malcolm Allison as his first team coach he knew his own health problems and said he would only do a few of years in the firing line, and if Malcolm made it he would recommend that he took over as Manager. Such was the impact of the Mercer/Allison combination on football that Uncle Joe became a national figure and at the end of the first season, 1966, when City finished as Second Division Champions and returned to the First Division, the World Cup was held at Wembley and Joe was a celebrity commentator and contributor to the television scene. He became a public favourite and City now had two personalities who both believed they could walk on water. All Joe's intentions of handing over went out of the window and Malcolm became frustrated and resentful of Joe's No. 1 image, when he considered he was the person mainly responsible for the obvious success. Like any other human beings both had flaws, but the combination worked whilst both had their feet on the ground. That all changed when resentment set in.

Nobody was closer to the action than myself and it is my considered opinion that, just like that other great partnership which eventually bit the dust, Brian Clough and Peter Taylor, neither Joe or Malcolm would have made City the fabulous team they became without the other. The partnership was a combination of Joe's human touch and tactfulness, particularly with players, and Malcolm's coaching methods and innovations. It proved a winner as City, after returning to the top flight, won the First Division 1967/68, FA Cup 1969, League Cup 1970 and Cup Winners' Cup 1970. However the sustained success led to Joe retaining his job for longer than perhaps anyone had imagined. It wasn't a problem to anyone while the silverware continued to find its way into our trophy cabinet, but it eventually became apparent that a 'situation' was arising which would damage the club immensely.

Much boring rubbish has been spoken and written about the subject of the schism which developed between our management team, but the facts are that City went to Malta in December 1971 for a break and to play local club Floriana on their sand pitch. The unfortunate conflict raised its ugly head when several of us were down at the Grand Harbour in Malta during our few days' rest. I was walking along with Joe and Malcolm, who as we were more or less on holiday had taken a drink at lunch time and suddenly started taking Joe to task about not handing over the reins. Joe started to give as good as he got and the matter became very heated. I told them to quieten down as the others would hear and that could have drastic consequences.

Malcolm was vehemently insisting that Joe had not been a success as Manager at Sheffield United and Aston Villa and Joe was responding by telling Malcolm he had brought him out of obscurity from Plymouth. It was all very unpleasant. Incidents not known outside the Club were bandied about and I told them to grow up and stop behaving like a couple of spoilt kids, and that they were doing neither themselves or the club any good and anything of this nature should be discussed in private and not when both were so hyped up. I was concerned for Joe who had a problem with tension and was clearly starting to suffer and I thought Malcolm was saying things he could later regret.

They cooled off a bit and I dropped behind them to allow what I hoped would be some sort of mutual reconciliation when they both calmed down. It did pass off on the face of things, but the relationship was never the same again. The next day Joe and I hired a car for a tour around the island and with me driving, as usual, spent most of the time having a heart to heart talk whilst trying to avoid the wartime potholes still evident on the Maltese roads. I told Joe straight that there was no way he could cope on his own and asked why on earth he would want to destroy a winning set-up, when a bit of give and take and a lowering of egos and swallowing of pride would keep both them and City at the top of the tree.

God would be in his Heaven, all would be well with the World, Bob would be your uncle, Fanny your aunt and Dick your best friend. It wasn't to be, and I will explain how the fallout unfolded in all its gory detail later.

At the time of writing this piece my wife Mavis and I are once again on holiday in Sliema, not more than a couple of hundred yards from where this unfortunate incident occured and it is so clear in my mind that it only seems a few months ago rather than nearly forty years. It was truly the end of a beautiful friendship.

It was while flying home from a break in Malta, that I learned, from the newspapers provided by British Airways, of the rotten news of Old Big 'Ead's demise. Brian Clough and I had a rather tenuous friendship over many years and although not often in each other's company we each gave as good as we got and seemed to enjoy the badinage and mutual piss taking. Despite being a couple of years older than Brian, and being the Chairman of a prominent club, I was still 'Young Man' to the autocratic Clough.

In 1978 a friend of mine, Geoff Karran, a big City fan and at that time the Chairman of a local cricket club on the Isle of Man, asked how much I thought Brian would charge to come over to the island and speak at the Centenary Dinner, if in fact he would even consider such a request. In those days I assumed even a thousand quid would be chicken feed to the great Clough, who at that time was in the full flow of his illustrious career, but I said we could only ask and promised so to do, knowing Brian was an avid cricket fan and a member of the Lord's Taverners. I contacted Brian and said the club was simply a small town cricket club, that it was a bit cheeky, they hadn't much money but would pay his airfare and accommodation in the first class hotel where the dinner was to be held and as a favour to me, would he consider the request.

A pause then, "Could they come up with a hundred pounds, Young Man?" Pause. "Cash."

I thanked him and said they would be delighted to welcome him, adding, "If you let me down or don't turn up, my son, I will personally come to Nottingham and kick the seven shades of s*** out of you."

"Send me the details," he concluded and down went the phone . . . end of conversation.

Clough was welcomed with open arms and when introducing him at the dinner, I mentioned we had asked him in order to save money on the fare, as no doubt he could walk across the Irish Sea and back. Bear in mind this was well before the hoary old chestnut about sponsored walks from Dover to Calais and it got quite a laugh but, by God, he got his own back. The first few minutes of his talk were spent taking apart football directors in general and me in particular, which obviously caused great hilarity among the guests. After the meal, everybody mingled and people saw another side of Brian Clough and I like to think that he made a big impression and many friends that evening.

That brings to mind an article in the paper in which his wife, Barbara, told a story about Clough returning home late one night and getting into their bed, which prompted her to exclaim, "God, your feet are cold!"

The Great Man responded, "It's all right, love, when we are in bed together you can call me Brian."

I passed the paper to my wife because my eyes were blurred.

MY FATHER and I did not always see eye to eye on some matters, but we were close friends and I maintained enormous respect for him and his attitude to life. He had very strong principles and a considerate manner, given by some the nickname 'The iron fist in the velvet glove'.

A rare compliment from Peter Swales stated that Dad was the best hatchet man he had ever known – if he sacked anybody he made them feel he was doing them a favour.

Dad rarely swore and I never heard him use bad language like the 'F' word beloved by some so called modern celebrities. He would call people 'Jossers' (a stables term, I assumed) 'Go to blazes' or 'Go and raffle yourself', or, more charitably, 'Poor fellow' where you or I might say 'Stupid sod' or similar. However his opinions and actions came across just as strongly, so I suppose it is all about what you say and actually do , rather than the way you say it. Rightly or wrongly, I have generally had a reputation for clear thinking and not being diverted from the main issue or bogged down and sidetracked with trivial details. I do not believe in hanging about in the mists of indecision when something has to be settled and a situation moved on and I came to the conclusion a long time ago that lack of decision is the undoing of many people, like those who abstain from voting on an issue for fear of what the 'winners' or 'losers' might say or do afterwards.

Eric Roberts, a sprightly 90 year-old, and I meet up from time to time for a chat and a spot of lunch and we make it our business to put the football world to rights. Eric read an early proof of this book and his enthusiasm encouraged me to continue with my efforts. He mentioned that some four weeks after joining the Liverpool board he was in charge of their reserve team who went to Maine Road to play City. Dad was responsible for City that day and welcomed Eric, showed him all around the ground, introduced him to all and sundry and made him most welcome. He has never forgotten the kindness and friendship extended to him that day.

The stories of my father are legion but this particular one is a tale that has been the subject of much plagiarism and I have known of authors and after-dinner speakers claim it as their own, but this is the true and original as recounted to me at the time by Joe Mercer, my father and recently confirmed in the City programme by Bobby Kennedy himself, who feels very strongly about the true facts of this matter.

City took a close season tour following the winning of the Championship in 1968 and played in Canada and the United States. City's Scottish full back Bobby Kennedy was in the party, in Atlanta at this particular time. Some of the players had been to a cinema the previous evening and there had been some local disturbance, serious enough for the police to strongly recommend that our party give the area a wide berth. The following evening Joe was watching television in his room when it was announced that Bobby Kennedy, the former President John Kennedy's brother, had been assassinated and Joe dashed round to my father's room with the news. Dad was sitting up in bed reading a paper when Joe burst in "Mr Chairman, Bobby Kennedy's been shot." My father, City to the roots, threw down his paper and stormed "God damn it, Joe, we told them they were banned from that street. What was the poor fellow thinking about, going down there. Good job we've got enough players with us."

Whilst recounting stories, there are a couple relating to Wembley and the Cup Finals and as the old place has now gone forever these are worth recording. At both the FA and Football League Cup finals each Club was invited to send two representatives, usually husband and wife to the match, the preceding reception and luncheon. John 'Tolly' Cobbold, Chairman of Ipswich, told me this one regarding his mother, Lady Cobbold, on the famous occasion when Ipswich reached the final for the first time in their history and most of the football world were supporting them. Harold Wilson was the Prime Minister and some hand-wringing flunkey approached her saying, "Lady Cobbold, would you care to be introduced to the Prime Minister?" Johnny's mother fixed the man with a haughty stare, held out her empty glass and said, "Thank him, but I would rather have another Gin and Tonic."

You sat more or less in alphabetical order of club name at the luncheon and as Mavis and I generally represented City for many years, she knew most of the people around us even if we did not meet up with some of them at games during the season. Bill Young of Manchester United and his daughter, Lorraine, John Moores of Everton and the Liverpool people were usually near neighbours and there was a fair amount of leg pulling at the expense of officialdom and other clubs. On this particular occasion my friend Eric Roberts had resigned as the Chairman of Liverpool and John Smith had taken his place. Smith was not my cup of tea as Roberts and I had been friendly for some years, he was a big Shankly man, well respected, and I'm afraid Smith gave you the impression that nothing had happened at Liverpool until he became Chairman and seemed to have a rather patronising attitude which irritated ,among others, both my wife and myself. John was the last to arrive at our particular part of the table and he shook hands with me and turned to my wife saying "Do I know you?"

Just how patronising can you get? We had been at a match or function in his company only a week or so previously and I was about to put him down with something like "Probably John, Mavis used to be the receptionist at the pox clinic", when my wife earned my undying admiration. Offering her hand, she looked him straight in the eye and said " Perhaps I bought some matches or bootlaces from your tray in Lime Street". Bill Young chuckled, Lorraine hooted and John Moores leaned across saying "You'll know Mavis next time, John".

> *'Every man who is high up likes to think he has done it all himself. The wife smiles, and lets it go at that.'*
> JM Barrie

Maybe John got his own back sometime later when City played at Liverpool. After the game, Mavis, Brenda Swales and the other City Directors wives went into the room where the visiting Directors wives were to be entertained. However, all the seats were taken and the tea finished, so they sat on the floor and eventually by the time more tea was brought it was too late as our ladies had to leave for home.

IF EVER Dad was ill or a bit under the weather any problems generally centred on his throat, which had been the focal point of his injuries from the gas attack near Ypres in World War One.

When he was 60 years of age he went into the Christie Hospital for radium treatment to his throat and returned home after a short stay and was virtually untroubled for the next twenty years. However in the summer of 1972 when he was eighty years of age and we were still playing golf together, even if I had to give him a shot per hole, he weakened a bit and admitted he was not at his best and by the start of the new football season in August he was tiring although in typical Alexander fashion, as my mother used to take the 'mickey' out of the male members of the family, he would neither admit to it or ask for sympathy.

City had qualified for the UEFA Cup and we played Valencia at Maine Road early in September and as President Dad hosted a reception for the Spanish officials prior to our match. Valencia were a good side and managed at that time by the World famous and revered Alfredo di Stefano, whom it was a pleasure to meet. The game was a 2-2 draw and we looked forward to the second leg at the end of the month.

I was out of the country for a few days and on my return I was told Dad was not at all well, so I travelled to his home on the Isle of Man to find him bed-ridden and just about on the way out.

We never wrapped anything up in our family and he said to me something I will always remember: "It's a bugger, Eric, they won't let me out of bed. The sooner I'm gone, the better. Get me burned and then get on with your lives. I know you will look after Mum and your young ones will be brought up properly. No regrets."

Dad rarely swore and I cannot recall him using that word before and he seldom called me Eric, usually Son or 'The Lad' if anything at all, so it was all a bit sad and final.

I took City to Valencia at the end of the month and after the match, which we lost 1-2, Valencia hosted a dinner party and the President asked about my Dad and wished his kind regards to be passed on to him. At the end of the evening the officials each were presented with a very attractive wrist watch, the face being a dark blue background and the Valencia crest in red and silver. Before the battery jobs, this was a wind up affair but very acceptable. On virtually all contact with European football clubs the President would be the 'top man' and the Chairman, if they had one, would be slightly ahead of the Manager. I can think of a few English clubs where that would not have gone down too well. Anyway, the President of Valencia was a magnate in the orange growing business, a pleasant man and good company and at the end of the presentation he made a short speech extolling the career of my Father, made a special presentation to me of a watch for Dad and wished me to give him the best wishes of Valencia and to tell him he was highly regarded abroad and not only in English football. Very flattering and I thanked him and promised to pass on the gift and the kind words.

When we arrived at Manchester Airport the next day Mavis was at the Terminal to meet me and as this was not our normal arrangement I knew something was wrong. There were tears in her eyes as she came up to me and before she could say anything I knew what had happened and that Dad had died. It transpired that it was just about the time the previous evening when the President had spoken and given me the watch for Dad. The players could see what had happened and Malcolm and Tony Book both came up to me with generous commiserations which were greatly appreciated. My two sons, Angus and Hamish, were given the watches as keepsakes or mementos.

At his memorial service people came from many parts of the country to pay their respects and Canon Paton-Williams, giving the address said, 'A remarkable man, one could say he gave his life to the promotion of a game, but it would be an understatement. This kindly little man possessed qualities of character that went beyond the limits of the turnstiles and left a lasting impression of kindness, humility and goodwill on all who were capable of appreciating what he was, he was true to himself, and therefore could not be false to any man. The world is poorer for his passing – something kind, something gentle, something good has gone out of life.'

It would be nice to think that one day, in the dim and distant future I trust, something similar could be said about me . . . but I very much doubt it.

> *'The worst misfortune that can happen to an ordinary man is to have an extraordinary father.'*

AFTER DAD died Chris Muir was brought back on to the Board by the new regime and became Swales' eyes and ears, his reward coming later when with Swales' powerful support, he was elected to Manchester County FA. At a celebration luncheon to mark City reserves winning the Central League Championship he lost his rag when I commented that "soup should be seen and not heard" and wanted to thump me. I had a quiet word I his ear and from that day I don't think we have crossed swords. In fact, to his credit, an asset was the interest we shared in the home growing of young players and Chris would brave all sorts of weathers and travel to watch our own or other clubs youth teams. He and I were really the only ones who had either interest or knowledge of such players, the other Directors generally only watching the first team. When I went on the Board there was a rota of matches with the Reserves who played in the Central League, usually on Saturdays and all the Directors, including the Chairman up to Peter Swales' time took charge of the Reserves four or five times a season depending on the size of the board.

It was an unwritten tradition in the league that a Director always acted as host at home games or traveled with the team to away ones. This rule was strictly observed throughout the Central League, although I remember going to Leeds United once when they were playing away somewhere in the FA Cup. Elland Road was practically deserted, although a groundsman or somebody got me a cup of tea at half-time. City had an exciting tie, but I would have been hung, drawn and quartered by our lot if I had not done my duty and attended the reserves.

Once I asked Secretary Walter Griffiths why Leeds and Derby County never seemed to be at the top of the hit parade within the football world. He could not provide an answer, other than that the situation went back years to before the War. One thing that stood out in my recollection was the visiting Directors used to arrive at your Boardroom before a game, pass the time of day, mention the weather, how you were both faring in the League or Cup and express hope (genuine or face value) that it would be a good game.

The first things some of the Leeds people asked would be "What will be the size of the crowd?" "How many programmes will you sell?" and suchlike financially orientated questions. Perhaps, judging by events over the past few years, they got their sums wrong. Oh well.

MUM SEEMED to lose interest after Dad went and she died nine months later. She had some very difficult times and family tragedies to cope with over the years and I suppose she had just had enough. By the beginning of the next football season I considered it would not be letting the family down if I did not go forward as Chairman after the Annual General Meeting. All the 'back biting', petty jealousies and even a dirty tricks campaign directed at one or two of us had sickened me and I have always had the strong view that sport, by it's very name and nature, is there to be enjoyed. Life is too short to waste some of it and as far as possible you should try and do the things that suit you and those nearest to you. Perhaps a bit old fashioned, but that's me I suppose. At least I don't wear socks with my sandals.

I had been giving some two or three hours a day to the job and thoroughly enjoying most of it. I would see the Secretary, a look around the ground, talk with Stan Gibson, perhaps have a cup of tea with the laundry ladies, some of the unsung heroines of the Club and go to the training ground. I was more or less self employed but it was increasingly difficult to find the time to cope with all the bits and pieces and a family business venture into the sports trade was starting to suffer from the about turn by Adidas, Umbro and other major manufacturers supplying the emerging super markets and emporiums who by the very nature of their requirements and buying power could afford to sell out at prices it was costing the small retailer to purchase. Eventually the death knell of the local sports outfitter as well as small retailers of general requirements.

Joe Smith was well out of the frame by now, but Swales and with his encouragement and both eyes on the shareholding, Simon Cussons was also champing at the bit. Simon was a nice lad, considered by most to be out of his depth in the football World but he loved the social side and Swales' rather backhanded compliment was that Simon had the position of Official Wine Selector to the Club. However, at a tounament at Huelva in Southern Spain we discovered Simon had hidden talent as a mental arithmetic genius. So it just goes to show, you never know what is round the next corner and in their lifetimes everybody is supposed to have fifteen minutes of fame. I thought probably that was his, but after selling his shares to a brewery, Simon became a County Councillor. Fortunately I had moved from Cheshire back to the Isle of Man.

I kept what I believed was a straight face and passed over the change gently in public, but several members of the Press could see through the situation and were understanding and complimentary, for which I was very grateful. Denis Lowe, of the *Telegraph*, had pulled my leg at Old Trafford during the previous season, saying 'When are you going on the Board here, you know more about the game than most people and they are short of young blood'.

Actually it was flattering to receive, indirectly, tentative approaches during the next week or so from two World renowned Lancashire clubs, two Midlands and one other Lancashire club. One of the Midlands pair was Coventry City, so Joe Mercer, who had moved on to Highfield Road by then, must still have rated me.

PETER SWALES was after the Chairmanship from Day One that he became involved in Manchester City, although he was bright enough to bide his time and avoid alienating many people inside and on the fringe of the game, realising that friendship and mutual goodwill generally prevailed within the League.

He and I were talking in his office one day, about the time Matt Busby and I were considering putting up for election to the Management Committee of the Football League, when he surprised me by saying his ambition was to be the Chairman of the Football Association. He said 'We'll go for a double header, me for the FA and you for President of the Football League'.

I could just see the other clubs going for that spot of nepotism. Maybe it was his sense of humour? Matt and I put up for election, opposing an elderly gentleman in his seventies from a Third Division club and who had been a member of the Committee since Adam was a lad. We came nowhere and this chap continued with the direction of football when he should have retired gracefully or been retired and treated with the respect he had earned, rather than the comments that had been passed around the League. I seem to recall being told that he had visited an Antiques Fair and an American had tried to buy him!

I still have some very complimentary letters of support from many of the top clubs of the time, but it was obvious that lower down they didn't want any more people from 'above' running the game. Understandable in some circumstances, but somewhat short sighted and prejudiced in the long run. I have made the point elsewhere that I believed, and still do for that matter, that younger blood was needed at that time and possibly fresh thinking could have altered the shape of 'things to come' and prevented many of the problems that blight our game today.

However, that was the end of any ambition I may have nurtured in that direction and, frankly,I was glad in later times that I had not gone down that particular path, although when you think of the money folk receive these days I could have done OK and would not have to caddy and wash cars to eke out my old age pension.

However, to return briefly to the Swales situation, he had the advantage of being much younger and active than most of the other representatives on the F.A., plus the driving ambition to succeed, which cannot be anything but to his credit. However in my considered opinion, shared later by others, City came a very poor second to his personal ambitions which became obvious to those working with him and was simply a vehicle for his progress. He frequently asked my opinion on games, players and managers, freely admitting there were many aspects of the game he did not either understand or about which he could not get an unbiased opinion.

Peter and I had what could be described as an armed truce. He was very clever in many ways and he recognised that he needed my goodwill, endorsement and apparent friendship whilst making his way in the game and among the clubs. Once he got elected to the FA, he started to become known and his journalist mentor and friend Paul Doherty, son of the legendary Peter and head of Granada TV Sport, ensured he obtained plenty of publicity, including a Friday evening TV spot tipping racehorses.

He made threats to me on several occasions, but knew I could blow the lid off and reveal numerous details and incidents which would not be to his advantage if it came to hey, lads, hey.

The only time he lost his temper with me was on the way back from a match in London when Peter, John Humphreys and I were travelling together in either his or John's car. We were talking about giving youngsters a chance instead of splashing out crippling transfer fees and he made some disparaging comment about our youth set-up. I said 'How would you know, you never see them'. He wasn't used to being told things like that. Look out, duck Alexander.

We stopped for a meal, which was silent and rather like the Last Supper and when we were walking back to the car John said to me that I'd been lucky that Swales had not gone off and left me behind. I retaliated and said he was the lucky one and if John had sided with him both of them and a few others would have been torn into little pieces in the papers should I have decided to open up. 'You and I have been good friends for a long time, John, but you are the Chairman of Umbro and it is obvious and you have told me how important the approval of Swales is to you. Well, if it is at any cost then I pity you'. Surprisingly, Swales and John were most considerate to me from then on and perhaps it could be said that this throw in was appropriate:

'Be careful, the toes you tread on today may well be connected to the backside you have to kiss tomorrow.'

Talking to contemporaries, such as old players, managers and retired officials, it does not appear to me that boards of directors these days have much, if any, input or say in the acquisition of players whereas in most cases it used to be the board, or in some despotic clubs the chairman, who discussed in great detail any forthcoming transfer and the effects on the club's finances and compatibility of personalities,

I dislike using the words 'In my time' or 'In the old days' as they reek of 'The good old days' syndrome, and whilst there were many good old days not everything that goes on in football today is bad, a hell of a lot is, but not everything.

Two examples regarding transfers come to mind, possibly illustrating my point about opinions and authority. As Manager of Manchester City, Tony Book wanted to sign Graeame Souness who was available from Middlesbrough for some £300,000. This matter came before the Directors and was discussed in great detail, more or less everybody making some comment or other. I had many contacts within the game at both playing and management levels, as did John Humphreys with his Umbro and Adidas connections, also Chris Muir although to a much lesser extent. Souness was a fine player who had a very successful career with Liverpool, but it was decided he was not for us and Book did not get his player. I get the impression these days that in some clubs the manager signs a player he wants, or is brainwashed by an agent into thinking he wants, and then tells the board.

The other transfer that caused well documented problems, widely opposed opinions and other disputes was the controversial arrival at Maine Road of Rodney Marsh. I was Chairman at the time, virtually a lone voice in the wilderness and opposed to Malcolm Allison's obsession for bringing Rodney to City. Contrary to Rodney's opinion that Malcolm wanted him as City's answer to George Best, I never heard that comment passed and at the end of the day, with all the eccentricities often displayed by brilliant players, George was a team player, something that was often lacking in Rodney's game. Tremendous skills but first and foremost an entertainer, something that does not win friends in the dressing rooms of professional football. Anyway, the Allison Fan Club led by Joe Smith and Co. triumphed and Malcolm, Secretary Walter Griffiths and myself were to fly down to London next day to sort out the matter. Joe Smith, who I believed loathed flying, was talked into coming with us to try and ensure I didn't wreck the transfer I considered unnecessary. As it happened, whether it was the flight down or the thought of the return flight, I don't remember Joe saying a word during the whole proceedings.

'Fate tried to conceal him by calling him Smith.'
Oliver Wendell Holmes

I was in some state of trepidation, Jim Gregory, the Chairman of Queen's Park Rangers, being a London car dealer and having the reputation in football as a pretty tough operator and with me being the 'country boy' from the sticks it all looked a bit one-sided. The top transfer at that time was Alan Ball to Arsenal for a reputed £220,000 and Gregory wanted £200,000 for Marsh. He would not budge and I, supported discreetly by Walter Griffiths, would not go that far. It was stalemate over some hours and I was beginning to enjoy myself thinking I was holding my own in such company. Eventually we came to a deal, Jim got his £200,000 which satisfied him and I insisted it included the 10%, that was 5% for the player and 5% to be put into the Players Provident Fund, administered by the PFA Honour was assuaged all round and Rodney travelled up next day to sign. Overweight and not up to the fitness standards very high on the priority list at City he struggled and to his credit is the first one to admit he virtually cost us the Championship that season, after City being out ahead with just a handful of games left to play. I quite liked Rod as a person and we were friendly during his time with City, in fact I have a photo somewhere which he gave to me, signed 'To my friend, the Chairman'. Not exactly a Hall of Fame collector's item but a nice gesture and appreciated.

An odd character, Rodney could be good company and I recall sitting next to him on a coach journey through the backwaters of Poland or somewhere and all the houses were painted different bright colours. This started a conversation and we found we had a mutual interest in art. On the other hand, he could do some irresponsible things like in Nigeria when we played there some of the Nigerian players had only recently started wearing boots, previously preferring bare feet.

We were sitting in the team coach outside the hotel in Lagos ready to go to the match and only the great Rodney was missing. Roy Bailey, the physio, was about to chase him up when who should appear at the top of the stairs in the hotel entrance but the man himself, in shorts and believe it or not barefooted. He made a big fuss of coming to the coach, apparently oblivious to the stones, filth and possible broken glass that was all around, all of which could have caused injury and possible premature finish to his playing career.

Contrast that attitude to convention with this one. When playing in the Midlands, City, United and several other clubs took a light lunch at Tillington Hall, near Stafford, before going to the away ground. This day I had City Reserves at Villa or Stoke or one of the Midlands clubs and when we entered the dining room United were already seated, having their pre-match meal before playing locally. Louis Edwards immediately invited me to join them at their table, but I went across, had a few moments chat and badinage then rejoined my lads. All the United players, including George Best who was not universally acclaimed for sartorial elegance, wore United club blazers, shirts and ties. The point being that if George Best could conform, surely Marsh could be expected to do the same?

Peter Gardner recently reminded me of Derek Potter's classic summing up of Rodney Marsh's attitude when he said 'Rodney Marsh will not be satisfied until he heads a penalty'.

Mention of Rodney Marsh and Alan Ball reminds me that a while before the Marsh business, I had a phone call at home one evening from Alan's dad, who I knew quite well and with whom I was friendly. It appeared Alan was wanting away from Everton and could use a few bob, the deal being at that time a transfer fee had 5% for the player and 5% into the kitty of the Players Provident Fund. Obviously anybody commanding a sizeable fee could do very nicely and one or two had quite a reputation for cashing in on this, shall we call it, facility.

Alan told me that Arsenal were interested and were talking around £220,000, but Alan Jnr. would be very willing to come to City, if we could come up with the money. I told him we would discuss it next day, which we did, and I can't remember why nothing went any further. I always rated Alan as a player, not as a manager but a player, and I would have been happy to have him at Maine Road. The only time I recall seeing him 'eradicated' from a game was at Villa Park in the 1969 F. A. Cup semi final when City beat Everton and David 'Tadger' Connor, not a great imaginitive player but a wonderful shadower and tackler with enormous stamina virtually tied himself to Alan's bootlaces and removed him from the game. To his credit Alan kept going, but obviously seethed with frustration. That was the day when Chairman 'Little Albert' went into the dressing room at the end of the game and said to centre half Tommy Booth, who scored the only goal, 'Well done, Tommy, now we've got to Wembley we will make a lot of money and then we will be able to buy some good players'. Dad had a lovely teasing sense of humour, nothing like as evil as mine can be sometimes, and when he told me that perhaps Tommy had not caught on to the leg pull I told him to watch out for some of the players getting their own back. I cannot recall it happening during the remaining three years of his life and certainly not by Tommy, who was always highly rated by both Dad and myself during the whole of his career, but one or two players tried to turn the joke round.

Over the years some of the speeches I have had to endure from people within the game made me realise some memories are as conveniently short as imagination is long. A few would have made a better living as science fiction authors. When you have witnessed the incident, situation or heard the actual words, it is an entirely different matter and sometimes you squirm or itch to tell the real facts. Which sometimes are funnier than the fiction.

> *'Men will confess to treason, murder, arson, false teeth or a wig. How many of them will own up to a lack of humour?'*

JOHN HUMPHREYS and I remained firm friends up to his untimely and sad death in 1979 at the early age of 49. A dreadful loss to his wife and family, his many friends and golfing partners and of course his business and it seems to me that it changed the direction of Umbro, which is now an American owned and operated giant..

There is little to be said for taking up further space on this topic, but some things needed saying and there were one or two incidents that cast a lighter side to the proceedings.

During the course of the first Board Meeting at which Swales presided as Chairman, he lit a cigarette, unheard of during a meeting at that time, tilted back his chair, put his feet up on the table and crossed his legs. A classic pose, one which would have made a good photo to replace the historic ones he had removed and thrown out when he became Chairman. Incidentally, most if not all of the pre-Swales era photographs of City's trophy-winning teams, historic events and so on were removed on his instructions, fortunately being discovered in a rubbish skip by a workman and rescued by director Ian Niven and rather acrimoniously restored.

I had forgotten this one but Harry Finlaison recalls that one away trip we were in a hotel for lunch and Simon Cussons must have crossed Swales in some way and instead of it being Simon's province, Swales decided he would order the wine. Receiving the wine list from the waiter, he studied it for an impressive couple of moments, handing it back with a nonchalant

"Yes, give us two bottles of that."

Simon obviously relished the opportunity to say gently, "I don't think that is too good an idea, Chairman, Chivas Regal is a fine whisky." Exit Swales.

Had it really been 'exit Swales' things would have been very different, but we were to suffer twenty years under the control of the self-styled 'Cincinnati Kid', a mythical gambler and poker player. Peter admired and joked with me several times that he tried to model himself on 'The Kid's style'. Certainly it was a very different situation when he took the Chair and after the enforced departure of Secretary Walter Griffiths, it was all change and Peter's friends and associates came in to replace the accountants, solicitors, travel agents and various suppliers who had worked with the Club for donkey's years. Out went British European Airways, BOAC, both of whom had keen City people in key positions such as Frank Bowskill at BEA and Joe Scott with BOAC and the agents Thomas Cook. I wonder how many of that era are still around to appreciate the rather ironic twist that sees the name Thomas Cook on the team and supporters shirts as the club's current sponsors?

Peter made what proved to be an ill-considered promise when appointing Ron Saunders a few weeks after taking the Chair.

Against advice he was so convinced Ron would be just the man he openly declared, "If he goes, I go". Saunders had some success at other clubs, but had a sergeant major attitude at City and the dressing room, containing quite a number of very well-known and articulate players, virtually rebelled at his style and approach to professional football. He lasted just six months and 20 years later, after 13 managers, a couple of relegations and one League Cup win Peter realised he was not top of everybody's Christmas card list and resigned from the club.

> '*There is no mistake in public leadership worse than holding out false hopes, soon to be swept away. The British people can face peril or misfortune with fortitude and buoyancy, but they bitterly resent being deceived or finding out that those responsible for their affairs are living in a fool's paradise.*'
> Winston Churchill

ELSEWHERE I'VE mentioned members of the Press, but one in particular must be singled out at this point, because I believe that as a token of long standing friendship and a tribute to departed merit, the following piece should be included. Alec Johnson, of *Express* and *Mirror* fame, had spent some years researching and compiling a book with a difference, generally about Manchester United and consisting of views and interviews with managers, directors, coaches, former players and people on the periphery.

Normally when in Manchester I would meet up with Alec in 'The Four in Hand' or 'The Old House at Home', watering holes close by where he lived in South Manchester. Alec was a keen sportsman in his own right, being among other things, the Royal Air Force Middle East Tennis Champion during his National Service in the early Fifties.

No mean performer at the bar either, and during the consuming of a pint or three of Guinness we discussed the state of football, authors, biographies and literature in general. Alec considered that I had some unique angles on the inside and background of the football world and was forever 'at me' to put my reminiscences down on paper.

Generally I changed the subject from soccer to his years of reporting golf and tennis with some remarkable and interesting interviews with famous stars. This fired him up and long discussions ensued on other sports and we left football behind. Unfortunately Alec took ill and never recovered, the book virtually finished but not completed and never published.

FATHER
Albert Edward Burns
Alexander.

SON
Albert Victor Alexander.

**DAUGHTER IN LAW –
'MUM'**
Emily Alexander.

GRANDSON
Albert Eric Alexander.

All Old Albert needs is
Steve McQueen riding
shotgun to complete
the opening of the
Magnificent Seven!

Grandpa driving the
United cup-winning Team
through Manchester,
1909.

CITY IN 1909.

GRANDPA WITH KING GEORGE V
Manchester City at Wembley, 1934.

CITY IN GERMANY, 1937
(Football Club Directors took their own wives in those days!) My Grandmother is centre front row with the handbag.

Young Albert (right), circa 1920 with the trademark bowler hat and City 'A' Team.

Dad in unison with Joe Mercer and Malcolm Allison.

Grandpa at Gatley Golf Club.

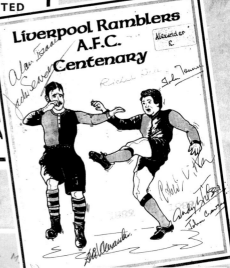

MANCHESTER UNITED
FOOTBALL C...
PROGRAM...
Wednesday, May 3rd

PRICE ONE PENNY

NUMBER 26

"GILGRYST" CUP FINAL

MANCHESTER UNITED "A...
MANCHESTER CITY "A...

Kick-off 6-30 p.m.

EARLY DAYS
Ronaldsway Airfield, 1938.

Gatley 'Gunner' at 15
(complete with baggy shorts and
laced collar).

The winning goal in Gatley's first
league game. (I really did send the
keeper the wrong way!)

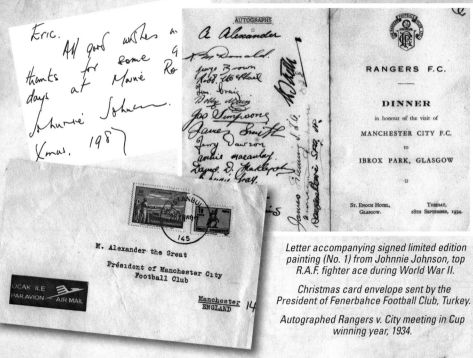

Letter accompanying signed limited edition painting (No. 1) from Johnnie Johnson, top R.A.F. fighter ace during World War II.

Christmas card envelope sent by the President of Fenerbahce Football Club, Turkey.

Autographed Rangers v. City meeting in Cup winning year, 1934.

Billy Meredith and Dad with bowler.

Manchester University Rag Day, 1951.
'NEW ORLEANS JAZZ'! (Politically incorrect
these days for black faces!)

GERMANY, 1937
A couple of interesting itineraries.

MUM.

AMERICA, 1968.

Dad loved this one of my young ones!
(LtoR) Dad, Angus (England), Louise (Brazil),
Hamish (City) and Jill (City Away).

1966 World Cup Programme.

Playing on the sand pitch, Malta, December 1971.

Great Barrier Reef fishing with Sidney Rose, self and 'green' Walter Griffith.

Isle of Man Millennium (1979). Presenting Isle of Man Official button hole commemorative badges to City players. (LtoR) Paul Power, Kenny Clements, Mike Doyle, Peter Barnes, Brian Kidd, Joe Corrigan, self and Roger Palmer.

17th hole at Castletown Golf Club.

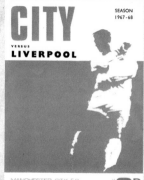

Climbing in the Mont Blanc area of the Alps 1949-1999.

First motor bike!

STILL GOT THIS ONE!

Sir Matt Busby.

Programme cover, part of publicity material designed by Alan Gordon and myself in the mid sixties.

WITH THREE LEGENDS Roy Clarke (L), Bert Trautmann (C) and Roy Paul (R) Hamish, with arm in sling, and Angus.

AUSTRALIA, 1970. (LtoR) Walter Griffith, Sidney Rose, self, W. H. & D. O. Wills, Manager & Australian Soccer Federation Official.

VILLA PARK, 1969
Dad with Tommy Booth after the F.A. Cup Semi-Final "... now we can buy some good players." (Tom autographed this one!)

With the Championship Trophy and the F.A. Charity Shield, 1968.

*Denis Law presenting me with International tickets,
which I had won in an Admiral competition.*

Presenting Dennis Tueart (L) and Trevor Francis (R) with joint 'Man of the Match' Awards.

'HOME'
Receiving a replica of the F.A. Cup from H.R.H. The
Duke of Kent at the Football Association Centenary
Dinner, 1972.

'AWAY'
Exchanging gifts in Nigeria, 1975.
My friend, City Secretary Bernard Halford keeps a
watchful eye on me.

THE SIGNING OF
RODNEY MARSH
His first steps on
Maine Road.

'BEFORE'
BMW to Vienna. Harry Finlaison, Alan Gordon and self.

'AFTER'
Back in Manchester with the European Cup Winners' Cup. Mavis, self, the Cup and Harry.

25 YEARS UNDETECTED CRIME
Receiving silver platter from Sir Bobby Charlton for 25 years on the Management Committee of the Lancashire Football League.

… judging by the number of 'life stories', some managers and players have had more lives than Henry, our cat.

Francis Lee becomes Chairman of Manchester City.

Alec Johnson (L) and 'Johnnie' Johnson, CB, CBE, DSO and two bars, DFC and Bar at the Bridge, Prestbury.

THE LAST SUPPER - (LtoR) Bill Bancroft (Blackburn Rovers), Sir Tom Finney (President), Michael Edelson (Manchester United), John Howarth (Secretary, Burnley), Ian Stott (Oldham Athletic), Barbara Howarth (Asst. Secretary), Dr. Milton Jeffries (Blackburn Rovers), Self (Manchester City). Final meeting of the members of the Football League Club Representatives on the Management Committee of the Lancashire Football League, prior to Academy.

Last Match at Maine Road Memories.

Personal letter of condolence to me from Prime Minister Edward Heath.

*Dad and Mum.
Golden Wedding time, 1969.*

(LtoR) John Humphreys, Frank Johnson, Self and Secretary Walter Griffiths.

LANCASHIRE FOOTBALL LEAGUE

ANNUAL REPORT 1995/96

Division One Winners 1994/95 – Manchester United A

Eric Alexander presenting the trophy to Eric Harrison

Just to show there is no prejudice!

JOHN BOND

ERIC ALEXANDER

*Centenary Cup Final, 1981.
City supporters club brochure.*

The following extract is here because it concerns two very good friends of mine, Alec and Sir Matt Busby, and was the result of an interview with me. It appears with the blessing and kind permission of Alec's widow, Sally, who says he would have been thrilled to bits to know that I had finally made it into print. So the following is my tribute to Alec and Matt ... the story is Alec's, and please bear in mind that it was written several years ago.

Matt Busby sipped his drink and considered the suggestion just put to him – why not quit the Manchester United Boardroom and become a Director of his former club, Manchester City? It seemed unthinkable that the man who built United into one of the most famous clubs in the world could contemplate leaving Old Trafford. Yet Busby was angry and frustrated. He felt his position at Old Trafford had become embarrassing and untenable. He had reached a point where he was giving thought to leaving the club he had practically built after the chaos of the Second World War. Busby had shaped the club's destiny before achieving his ultimate dream by winning the European Cup in 1968. Finally, he had moved into the Boardroom three years later, but by 1975 Busby had reached his nadir at United.

Busby was sitting with Eric Alexander, the prominent Manchester City Director and former Chairman of the Maine Road club, whose family had always been close to Busby. It was Eric's father, the likeable 'Little Albert' who had played a major role in bringing Busby to City from his Scottish club, Bellshill, and considered him a shrewd and talented player but lacking in pace for an inside-forward and moved Matt to wing half from where he became a Scottish International and had an illustrious playing career. Eric Alexander realised as he chatted that Busby was bitterly hurt and dejected. "I sensed as I listened to him that this wasn't the usually enthusiastic Busby sitting in the Maine Road Boardroom with me after a Derby game," says Alexander. "Matt was dejected and gloomy. We often sat together at matches and always had an excellent relationship."

It was well-known in Manchester soccer circles that all was not well behind the scenes at Old Trafford. They knew Matt was unhappy because he had failed in his attempt to get his son, Sandy, onto the United Board with him. Busby had been all-powerful as Manager. His word was law, but this was a different set-up. Soccer was now big business and those with the major shareholding ruled the roost. Chairman Louis Edwards held zealously to his position of control. The Boardroom was the seat of power and reputations counted for nothing. Busby the Scottish Patriarch had been a Grand Master in the art and strategy in handling players . . . manipulating them to extract the finest and most impressive results. "He was hard as iron when he felt it was necessary," says the former United midfield warrior Pat Crerand. "Players were putty in his hands. He knew how to handle his team . . . how to get the best out of it by keeping everyone just that little bit on edge . . . never quite sure what was coming next. Matt was the supreme motivator, but he could also be ruthless when he felt people weren't giving him 100%. That was what he demanded all the time and that is why he was so incredibly successful". But Busby could not command that sort of control in the Boardroom.

"Clearly he was bitterly upset at the way things were going for him personally," says Alexander. Many at Old Trafford believed Busby's aim had been not only to get his son Sandy on the Board, but to be himself made Chairman - the last great triumph of his magnificent football career. "I think he felt he was being ignored and had no real part to play in the club's affairs" says Alexander. "How are thing goings, Matt?" I asked him. He stared in his glass and muttered, "So so." He knew I was aware of his unhappiness so I suggested why not think about coming over the Maine Road as a Director. After all, I reasoned, he had started his career with City. I said to him "You can always come back to Maine Road. What a homecoming that would be." Matt was quiet for a few seconds and then looked up and said to me, "Aye, Eric, now that's a thought." Alexander had aroused a feeling of rich nostalgia that tempted Busby to prove a point by returning to the first club of his career in English football. Alexander, whose keen sense of humour always lurked only fractionally below his attitude to life, mused, "That would cause a hell of a shock at Old Trafford. But think of the reception you will get from the Maine Road faithful. They will go crazy."

Busby nodded, smiling thoughtfully. It was clear Alexander had set the great man thinking. But then Busby asked, "What about Peter, what would be think about it?" That was a crucial reference to the then City Chairman,

Peter Swales, yet another ruthlessly ambitious man in the world of soccer. Swales ruled Maine Road with a grip of steel, but his Directors although powerless because of Swales' massive shareholding, were desperately looking for a benefactor to achieve a new and more exciting City outlook. Yet Swales was all powerful. Alexander gave a shrug of indifference. "Bugger Him," he said, hitting an adventurous note, "Just think what the fans will say . . . it will set Manchester football on fire". Busby told Alexander he would leave the matter with him to see what reaction would be forthcoming. When it was put to Swales, the City Chairman grimaced saying "He would never come back here, would he?" Says Alexander, "But he knew that if Matt was to set foot in the City Boardroom then his position as Chairman would have been under threat". Busby heard on the soccer grapevine that Swales would oppose the suggested switch of camps by the great Scotsman and that was enough for Busby, who had no intention of being the centre of a possible squabble between the clubs. He indicated to Alexander that he had decided to 'let the matter drop'. That was the end of a possible move that might have reshaped City's destiny.

"Had Matt decided to come over, he would have been welcomed with open arms by practically everyone at Maine Road, but Swales clearly saw him as a threat to his own position. Matt would have given us an extra dimension. With his vast experience and prestige he could have helped reshape the club's playing fortunes. He was such a legendary figure that he would have made someone like Swales pale into insignificance and Swales wasn't going to let go his grip on the club. Pity" says Alexander.

Had Busby been given his chance at his old club it is fascinating to imagine what he might have achieved. Yet happily for United, Busby finally settled down again and enjoyed the massive success which arrived at United when Chairman Martin Edwards brought Alex Ferguson to Old Trafford.

Edwards insists: "Matt and I never exchanged cross words. He was a wonderful person and possibly the greatest Manager ever", adding "Matt's advice was always welcomed. He played a prominent role regarding the appointment of most new managers until the point where we brought in Alex Ferguson". Edwards reveals Busby's great original hope, after Wilf McGuiness had to be replaced, was to persuade the great Celtic and Scotland Manager, Jock Stein, to take over the Old Trafford reins. "We thought it was all settled" says the United Chairman, "I went to my father's house and Stein was there sitting on the settee with Matt and my father. They were all very excited, and Jock was to go back to Scotland to settle matters up there and then it was to be announced he would be joining us. But it all fell through because Jock's wife, Jean, wouldn't move south. It was a big disappointment all round."

It is ironic that Stein chose Alex Ferguson as Assistant Manager when he was in charge of the Scottish International team. Ferguson had a tremendous regard for the Celtic legend and they had an affinity in loving to theorise for hours on end about the game. So indirectly Stein did play a small part in United's return to former greatness for Ferguson admits that much of the Celtic and Scotland Chief's expertise has rubbed off on him and has stood him in good stead.

"It was a wonderful experience working alongside Jock," Ferguson says, "We had a terrific relationship and I learned a lot from him regarding tactics, handling players and getting the very best out of them."

Says Jim Rodger: "Just think what football knowledge was passing between them? It was remarkable. Here was the Master giving Ferguson the vital experience and encouragement that was to take him to the top. Don't ever think that Alex did not listen and learn . . . exactly the opposite . . . he had how own plan. It was especially one of attack. But most of all it was about the sheer will to win he wanted to instill into every player in his squad. That was the Busby passport to victory . . . I felt that Ferguson had brought an exciting approach into top football at that time".

Busby remarked, having put his previous Boardroom disappointments behind him, "Alex has an adventurous attitude and wants to play attacking football. That is the way I want to see this club go forward. It has been our by-word." Ferguson was to use all this expertise to reach out for the chance he wanted more than anything - to manage Manchester United. Busby with his future finally resolved to remain at Old Trafford was clearly pleased that it would be another ambitious young Scotsman who would be trying to follow in his footsteps. The job of managing United has always seemed just too much for all his predecesssors. "He never interfered, but was always there if I wanted advice" says Ferguson firmly. "He was simply a wonderful father figure to have around the club".

It must have jogged Busby's memories when Ferguson began to turn United into the sort of team he had built when he first came to Old Trafford. Busby joined United as Manager on Monday, 19th February 1945. Yet at that point he was still a Company Sergeant Major Instructor while also a cunning midfield player with Liverpool, plus being Scotland's skipper. Matt had turned down the chance to become No. 2 to Liverpool's Manager, George Kay, but United's bubbly and adventurous Secretary, Walter Crickmer, who had also been carrying on managerial duties at Old Trafford told Matt, "This is your big chance. You can be the complete Boss". Busby was 34 – quite young even by today's managerial standards, but the wily Crickmer knew they had landed a massive catch. He revealed, "Busby had a number of offers, but we were determined to get him," and then added prophetically: "He will build up the team and put it where it belongs . . . right at the top." United's then Chairman James Gibson had urged Crickmer to persuade Busby to settle his football career with United. The success of their plan was to prove an astronomical triumph - Busby achieved his dream by winning the European Cup.

That is the end of Alec's piece, but an additional few words from me. Sir Alex Ferguson emulated this tremendous achievement and scored an emphatic Treble with the FA Cup and Premiership title in 1999 and then lifted Europe's most prized trophy once again in 2008. A vociferous supporter of the Labour Party, he received his Knighthood literally within minutes of completing the third leg of that fantastic '99 treble. Mind you, when you see some of the honours handed out these days in football and life in general, Sir Alex has certainly done the business over a considerable period of time and unlike some others has not been a five minute wonder. Love him or dislike him, he must be the most successful manager of all time. Maybe if he hadn't got his 'Sir' for football possibly he would have got one for services to the chewing gum industry.

THINKING OF Alec Johnson reminds me that one of my boyhood heroes was 'Johnnie' Johnson or to be correct Air Vice Marshal J.E. Johnson, CB, CBE, DSO and two Bars, DFC and Bar, the top RAF fighter pilot of World War II. A fantastic record, all Johnnie's 39 victories were against fighter aircraft and I believe he was the only Ace never shot down. I met up with him through business and we became good friends. His support from childhood for Stockport County was about the only thing I could rib him about, but we went to many matches together and he really enjoyed his football, probably more so than if he had watched County all his life. On an occasion when Peter Swales was having a hard time from the fans, somebody threw an egg which hit Peter smack on the back of his hat. Johnnie turned to me and said, "Bloody Hell, Alec, that was a bloody good shot. If Douglas (Bader) had been as good, he'd have doubled his score." He always joked that his great friend and fellow Ace had to 'spray' his shots to hit anything, whereas Johnnie had learned to shoot rabbits as a young boy in the hills of Derbyshire and was a crack shot.

Alec Johnson knew of my friendship and confessed he, too, was an avid fan of Johnnie and asked if we could meet up sometime and fulfill a long standing ambition of his own. He promised he had no intention of turning it into an interview and we all met up for lunch a month or so later. An interesting and very enjoyable two or three hours. Sadly, that proved to be the last time I saw Johnnie and almost the last time I saw Alec. I seem to be forever turning up twists of fate, coincidences or call them what you will, but both Alec and Johnnie died on the same day some three months later.

MALCOLM ALLISON was a complex character, misunderstood by many people – mind you he didn't help himself in many ways. He almost encouraged controversy, but contrary to some popular beliefs he was not money orientated. Malcolm and I are friends and I see him fairly regularly at City home games and although he is not a well man and his memory is very vague, we still discuss the game and incidents he can recall. Probably he was the best coach of individual players that I have ever worked with and his perception of potential was remarkable. Unfortunately he had a penchant for getting things right and then wanting to move on to something seemingly outrageous in what appeared to some of us an effort to prove a point to himself as much as others.

At the City Centenary Dinner in 1994 he, his wife and I were the last of the guests to still be around in the hotel lounge during the early hours of the morning and we were discussing past events when he said something that I shall never forget and which made me feel good. Talking about his return to City as coach in 1978 under the management of Tony Book, he said if I had still been Chairman I would have understood what he was trying to achieve and in his words, "You had the patience and understanding to wait a 100 years if necessary, but Swales wanted instant success at any cost". That was very kind of him. I told him that if I had still been Chairman, probably he would not have got the job. We are still friends.

'Patience is something you admire in the driver behind you, and scorn in the one ahead.'

The famous millstone that hung around Malcolm's neck was the Steve Daley transfer from Wolves. He'd been interested in the player for some time, believing that he could improve Steve's potential and agreed a transfer fee of some £650,000, which was quite a bit in those days as there had only ever been a couple of million pound transfers at that point. To his horror Swales and the Wolves Chairman got in on the act and between them went up to a record £1,430,000 or thereabouts.

This enormous fee sickened Malcolm and a number of us. Also poor Steve Daley suffered with the title of the most expensive player on the planet and his form dropped accordingly. I had watched him on three occasions, including once at Old Trafford which was a fitting test and I was of the opinion that his style flattered to deceive, but of course that was just a Director's opinion. However we signed him and I felt sorry for the lad who did not live up to the expectations promised by the size of the eventual fee.

Whether he realised it or not, and whether he would ever admit it or not is certainly in question, Malcolm could not handle being manager. A superb and innovative coach, probably he would have deserved a 'legendary' title had he stayed downstairs in the dressing rooms of football and left the 'upstairs' work and responsibilities to others more suited to that side of the game. I say 'game' because it was a game in his time, as opposed to the business of today. I sometimes wonder how some of the great managers of yesterday would cope with the financial pressures of the current times.

I recall one famous International forward who became a fairly successful manager in the Fifties whose usual contribution to the pre-match scene was an instruction like "I want to see how fast their centre-forward can limp."

IN THE early 1970s City embarked upon a close season tour of Greece and the owner and President of Olympiacos was the ship owner Christos Goulandris (hope I've spelt that correctly) who was reputed to be wealthier than Mr Onassis. Goulandris was a friendly man who was good company, but had the terrible affliction of Parkinson's Disease which meant he had a servant, more like a bodyguard it seemed to me, with him most of the time. He was quite a heavy smoker and at times when his 'shakes' were really bad this man had to get his cigarettes out and light his fag for him. Christos decided he would like City to play an additional game whilst in Lagonissi and I put it to the players, who didn't really want to play again but when I told them I might disappear never to be seen again if we didn't play ball, so to speak, they showed their loyalty by offering to play if they got £100 each in cash for the privilege. I sat across the table from the great man and his bodyguard. Suddenly my confrontation with QPR's Jim Gregory paled into insignificance.

Despite being one of the World's wealthiest men Goulandris would not cough up the money and, although having a nasty feeling I might finish up over the side of one of his tankers with lead weights round my ankles, I would not back down either. We agreed to differ and we did not play the extra game, staying friendly and Christos told me later he was interested to see how far or how long I could resist in the confrontation. He and his wife, who was educated in England and was a great Glenn Miller and Tommy Dorsey fan, invited the whole of our party to their home for a day and we all had a great time. Goulandris and his brother had their tankers built in Japan and had two 'yachts' built as part of the order, but Christos found he hardly used his and sold it and bought a hillside, which his wife had irrigated and cultivated, creating a wonderful family estate. Joe Corrigan indulged in some fancy diving off the rocky headland which formed part of the grounds and we wondered if we would ever see him again. He was a great swimmer and he really enjoyed himself. We were taken on board the brother's yacht, which was about as big as the Isle of Man Irish Sea ferry, and the whole day was quite an experience, like something you imagine Hollywood is all about or perhaps your Lottery dreams.

WHILST I find it comparatively easy to talk and discuss people, incidents, opinions and so on in person, at times I've found it difficult to put these subjects in writing, where they can be read or interpreted in differing ways. However, I've done my best and, as I said in the preface, will let the facts speak for themselves. Distasteful though it is to my story, the following event shaped the future and no doubt the rest of my life and consequently the lives of my family. Whilst I don't wish to bore you by droning on about its significance, the next page or two is essential to the unfolding of Manchester City's history from the highpoint of 1970.

City winning more or less everything except the Grand National around that time brought the simmering ambitions of Chris Muir and his friends to the surface, which led to considerable friction among sections of the shareholders. Together with coach Malcolm Allison believing Muir was the chief reason for the club's revival in the mid-Sixties and success thereafter, this situation probably provoked the most disastrous period in the club's history.

There was never a dull moment with Allison around. After those spectacular successes of the late Sixties there were at least four occasions when Malcolm was 'tapped up' by other clubs including Rangers, Coventry City and a massive temptation from AC Milan. In that particular instance City could not stand in his way and Dad went on record as saying "who could blame anyone for considering a salary of £20,000 per annum?" – a King's ransom in those days. City sought £10,000 compensation for Allison's defection as his contract ran for another three years. Malcolm flirted with the Italians for a week or two and then, like the prodigal son, returned to Maine Road saying, "How do you explain that human ties mean more to you than money? People say that Joe and I get emotional about our football, but I believe that to enjoy any kind of success you have to pour your emotion into a game that can be so cruel. What is the point of making a lot of money if you've forgotten how to live?"

My father, described in a contemporary newspaper as 'the only man in England who can frighten Malcolm Allison', was disappointed Malcolm did not keep his promise to let him know first of his decision to stay with City, instead choosing to tell a newspaper, but did not make an issue of it, rejoicing that his staying would delight both the players and the supporters. He also said, "God help anyone who tries it on us again".

Unfortunately those words proved to be prophetic in an unforeseen way, when Malcolm became frustrated at not taking over as Manager from Joe Mercer who retired in 1972, when he considered he was the one who had done all the work on behalf of City.

Allison learned that shareholder Frank Johnson was eager to sell his considerable stake in the club in order to move abroad. Allison frequented a pub run by a very enthusiastic City fan, Ian Niven, and put it about that he wanted a man with about £100,000 to buy out Johnson's shares. Niven was connected with a chap called Joe Smith who had become wealthy from a double glazing venture and the promised incentive of becoming Chairman of what was at that time one of the top three League clubs fired up the imagination of both Joe and his wife. It was put about that Joe had been a poor boy who had supported City since a child and could never afford the entrance fee and all that sort of 'sob publicity'. It was obvious from Day One that Joe knew virtually nothing about City, or football, but he had the required money and the Directors were powerless to prevent the sale to him of Johnson's shares. In view of stirrings during the successes of the mid-Sixties, on joining the Board I had queried Frank Johnson about protecting the club from possible disruption, asking him if there was any method by which departing Directors could be compelled to offer the first opportunity to purchase shares to their colleagues in what at that time was a private limited company. My genuine question was laughed off with Johnson's characteristic 'embarrassed' giggle and I was told that no such provisions could be put in place. Actually, Frank did not seem to have much of a clue about football, despite having quite a number of years on the Board. He was particularly soured up at never becoming Chairman and originally we other Directors wondered if that was behind his eventual actions.

Rumblings started around November 1970 when City were in full flow, highly respected and heading for further successes. The Cussons family from the soap industry held a large block of shares and they were now in the name of Simon Cussons, a young man in his mid-twenties who was employed by the firm, various stories abounding as to how he became involved in the consortium attempting to take over City, and in view of later events I believe the most likely one being the promise of becoming President at some future time.

In the light of lost and untraceable shares, the combined Smith and Cussons shareholdings eventually constituted a majority, but the Board still had the opportunity to increase their strengths by co-opting two Directors of their choice and at the end of the season, around April 1971, Peter Swales and Robert Harris came to the club. Later in the year Joe Smith and Simon Cussons joined the Board and the face of the club had irreperably altered almost overnight. Actually, had it not been for the horrible consequences to Manchester City Football Club, which would last a generation, the whole business could have been the scenario for a farce or an Ealing comedy. In view of those consequences it was more like the basis for a Hammer horror movie:

SCRIPT
Malcolm Allison (from an idea by Peter Donaghue and Chris Muir based on a fantasy by Frank Johnson)

DIRECTOR
Michael Horwich

CO-DIRECTOR
Peter Swales

PRODUCER
Joe Smith

ASSISTANT PRODUCER
Ian Niven

BEST BOY
Simon Cussons

EDITOR
Chris Muir

ACADEMY AWARD NOMINATION FOR SUPPORTING ACTRESS
Dorothy Smith

Strange how things change around in life, Ian Niven and I have been friends for years and he told me not long after the Smith business, that had he known my father and I beforehand there was no way he would have got involved in the takeover, although he relished his directorship. Around the time it became obvious that Joe could never handle the top job his wife went off with somebody else. Joe's attitude changed considerably and he eventually married a very nice lady, Connie, who seemed to have a great influence on his lifestyle. Joe and I eventually became friendly, as did our respective wives and younger daughters. He found his niche in the football world when he set up an Executive Dining Suite at the Club and acted as host, something he was good at and enjoyed.

At the time of the Smith/Cussons arrival the Board was restructured and Dad, worn out having worked tirelessly to try and stabilise the club, relinquished the Chair. Obviously even the new Directors recognised his invaluable contribution and standing in the football world and following in his father's footsteps he became the second President of the club. If I say it myself, I know he was pleased and satisfied for the remaining twelve months of his life that I was made Chairman. It was realised by all that Joe Smith could not cope or handle it and accepted grudgingly that I was the one with the knowledge and the goodwill of most of the officials in football, plus the mutual respect and confidence of many managers and players.

To put one of the new people in authority would no doubt have alienated most of the other clubs, as in those days unlike recent times when clubs are subject to takeover and wholesale changes overnight, the Boards of Directors of virtually all Football League Clubs stayed fairly constant with only occasional change.

There was close friendship and fellowships between most of the clubs and the majority of us knew each other quite well, which generally meant that you wanted to beat them on the day, but you made light of it and, in most cases, generally accepted the result with good grace. Because it was only a few years ago, an example comes to mind and perhaps illustrates the point. Arsenal were in full flow and the visitors to Maine Road, going four goals up after some twenty minutes. City were no mugs but could not counter the brilliance of the whole Arsenal team, and the word 'team' summed up the situation. At half-time I spoke to the then Arsenal Vice Chairman, David Dein, and said how much I had enjoyed and admired his team's performance, although I hoped we would get back into the game in the second half. He looked quite surprised and asked if I really meant what I had said, adding that it was incredible how our supporters had cheered and clapped both teams off the field at the break as in many cases the crowd would be leaving for home in disappointment and disgust. I told him it was like watching the Real Madrid team of the Sixties and that City fans were renowned for their sporting attitude.I didn't add that it was an essential ingredient after some of the things that had happened over the past 30 years.

We got back into the game in the second half and gave as good as we received, so it finished up a cracking match which Arsenal deserved to win, but City had proved worthy opponents and anybody with a true appreciation of football must have had an exciting afternoon.

The fallout of the takeover continued when, towards the end of the 1971/72 season, Allison and his admirers on the Board decided they did not want Joe Mercer to have the title 'Manager' in any connotation, as in their opinion it detracted from Malcolm's position and kept Joe as the ostensible top man. You have to remember that football club directors could not be paid at that time, otherwise to my simple mind it would have solved all the board-generated problems if Joe had been made a Director and been paid a salary. I am certain this would have satisfied all parties and avoided considerable ill feeling and long term problems at the Club. I spent ages trying to convince the other Directors that Joe should stay, even if it was only for his public image and popularity which was all to the advantage of Manchester City. Nothing doing, but eventually they reluctantly agreed that if Joe himself could come up with a title which was acceptable to both the Board and Allison he would be able to continue at the Club. I went round to Joe's house the next morning and sat at the breakfast table with both Joe and his wife Nora. I told him I had supported him and pleaded with him to accept the situation for both his own benefit and that of the club. All it needed was a little give and take to see the team he and Malcolm had created so successfully back on the track. I left it with them both to consider a title that would be acceptable to all parties and departed thinking I had worked a miracle to keep Joe in a job and at City, even if it had hardly increased my popularity with the other Directors and rather put my position at risk.

Another of my interests in life is motor cycle racing, particularly road racing as promoted in the Isle of Man and Ireland. For over fifty years I have marshalled at the TT Races and the Manx Grand Prix, originally as a Marshall and currently as Chief Sector Marshall, and even a short spell helping out as Chairman of the Association. One day perhaps I will realise that life is far less complicated and pleasurable in the background rather than the forefront. We left it that Joe was to let me know what he had decided and I headed off to the TT Races for the next two weeks. On getting to my cabin on the boat for the journey back a fortnight later, I picked up the paper and as usual started from the back page: 'Mercer sent to Coventry' blared the headline. I could hardly believe what I was reading, not exactly unusual in the papers but this really hurt.

'Well, f*** me gently,' I thought, 'after all I've done and risked for him.' According to the article Joe had been forced out of City with no support from within and Coventry City had been negotiating with him at the time I went to see him trying to help him out. I was really hurt over this let down and it was some time before I got some respect back for him. Joe always said he worked hard at being popular and he did it very well, but this incident and the way I had stuck my neck out for him virtually cost me the Chairman's position at City. The next Board meeting was all "we told you so" etc., from the other Directors although I stayed in the Chair for a further season.

Although I was disappointed in the way it had been carried out behind the scenes, Joe and I remained friends for the rest of his life, which unfortunately was all too short. Nora still comes to the City matches and shares her toffees with me.

Back to the Malcolm Allison saga: one evening at the end of March 1973 Ray Bloye, the Chairman of Crystal Palace, rang me at home – I don't know how he got my number – asking if they could approach Malcolm with a view to taking over as manager at Palace. I know I play the country boy, but am I really that green? I had heard on the football/journalistic grapevine that Palace had been tapping up Malcolm and it came as no surprise, although I pretended to be indignant and rather shocked. It actually seemed to me a great way out of the problems we were encountering and after blustering a bit and mentioning words like 'compensation' I promised to discuss the business with the Board the next day. Allison's allies were shocked, but he moved to Palace later that day.

If only he had stuck to coaching and not wanted the Manager bit Malcolm would have had it made for years to come, but he moved to several clubs both home and overseas and never had any real success and suffered domestic and serious health problems. We promoted coach Johnny Hart to manager and with his background as player, coach and being a 100% City man, we looked forward to the next season with some rejuvenated hopes.

Secretary Walter Griffiths was the next target for the new City System. Walter was highly respected and efficient, in fact regarded by many as probably the best secretary in the Football League. However, before my time on the Board there had been some 'spat' between Walter and Swales' journalist pal Paul Doherty. I never knew the details, but Paul was banned from Maine Road and eventually with Swales gaining more and more influence over the other Directors, Walter was more or less forced into a corner and resigned. Bernard Halford was Secretary at Oldham Athletic and he was brought to City, with Walter eventually going in the opposite direction. Bernard has been at City for over 30 years now and is highly regarded both at the club and within football. 30 years must be heading up for some sort of record. Indeed Secretaries seem to have far longer lifespans than managers. During my lifetime City have had 24 managers and only three secretaries. Sometimes you wonder if secretaries know too much for chairmen to sack them.

ANYWAY, ENOUGH of all that sort of stuff, it had to be mentioned, but let's get on to far more interesting and agreeable topics. Each year the Football Writers' Association host an annual dinner in London on the Thursday evening prior to the Saturday FA Cup Final and if you were invited it was because of one of four reasons: A) you had been cooperative over the past season; B) a journalist was hoping to squeeze some scoop out of you; C) you were considered 'one of the boys' or D) you were just plain lucky. From whichever direction the invitation arrived, certainly in my case it was very welcome and gratefully received as the Football Writers' 'do' was always a great night (apart from the time Billy Connolly was at his filthy 'best' and many of us repaired to the bar). It is a great occasion on which to meet up with old friends. The main function of the evening is to announce and present the Award for the Player of the Season, a very pleasant event and certainly years ago one which was normally obvious and non-controversial. Generally a player had been outstanding for his playing ability, his leadership or perhaps his example to others over a long career and the dinner was a fitting precursor to the Cup Final and it did give you the Friday to detoxify. Although I remember when City were in the Final in 1969, John Humphreys and I got back to our hotel about 3 o'clock in the morning, caught the 7 o'clock Pullman back to Manchester in time to travel back with our families, the other directors, all the staff and sundry odd bods who we took as guests to the Final on the chartered Pullman to Euston.

John was not a great eater as I have explained elsewhere and a lasting impression of my old pal is leaving Watford station around 0725 hours on the way up to Manchester on the day in question and the steward or catering attendant taking breakfast orders, me starving as usual and ordering 'the lot', Humphreys dozing and endeavouring to recover before meeting up with his family, opened one eye and said "One kipper, please", closed his eye and then added what to me in the circumstances was the hilarious punchline, "Medium rare".

But on to the Writers Dinner of 1973 and during the afternoon I was in the bar of the Russell Hotel (surprise) in the company of several players and newspapermen (bigger surprise) and I believe, Bobby Charlton, somebody else from United and Denis Law. The others cleared off, probably it was Bob's round, leaving Denis and myself to reminisce. You know, I've never forgotten Jack Charlton saying at Middlesborough's Centenary Dinner, "The last time 'our kid' got his fags out, a cigarette card of Stanley Matthews fell out". Denis was fed up having just been told by Tommy Docherty that he was released and was finished at Old Trafford. I did not know of any background and this news was quite a surprise to me and I asked him if he had any plans in mind. It seemed Blackpool had got wind of the situation and had made Denis a tentative approach, but he was off up to Aberdeen for a holiday on his home territory and would take some private time to think about any future for him in the game. I had known Denis since my Dad, who was friendly with Bill Shankly, and Les McDowall brought him to City from Huddersfield Town and we talked quite openly about his fitness and enthusiasm for the game. To cut the story short, after buying him another drink (he is from Aberdeen, you know) I said "Right, Denis, let's not piss about, how do fancy playing the rest of your football at City?" And the rest as they say 'is history'.

Actually not quite, Denis was very interested but wondered if Johnny Hart would share my opinions as I was only the Chairman and Johnny was the new manager. Don't forget, Dear Reader, that I come from a generation where Chairmen, like the children of those times, were seen and not heard. Well, not in public, the newspapers or on television. Johnny was staying in the hotel and I promised Denis we would discuss the situation on the spot. Finding Johnny, I told him of the conversation and his response was "Denis, what a ****ing player". Of course John had been at Maine Road when Denis played for City and like everybody else had seen the talent that had been nicked by the Italians, but more of that particular skullduggery elsewhere. Then John's face dropped, "What will everybody say, my first signing as manager and it's a hasbeen on a free transfer?"

"Denis will kill you if he hears that, he's still on the ball and I guarantee he would just love to stick two fingers up to Tommy Doc. Come on Johnny, it will be a sensation. Pity you can't announce it tonight."

The persuasive powers of alcohol worked and I got Johnny round to my way of thinking. He met up with Denis during the evening and I reckon that, even at London beer prices and out of my own pocket, that was probably the cheapest and certainly one of the greatest and most satisfying of my accomplishments on behalf of City. Denis received a hero's welcome back to Maine Road and to rapturous applause scored two goals on his debut. Of course famously he was involved in that derby match at the end of the following season at the end of which United were relegated. Denis scored his cheeky backheel goal to win the game for City, although United's fate was already sealed as other results meant they were down whatever the result.

IT'S SURPRISING how many people get facts wrong, either unintentionally or otherwise, and it can be very irritating when you are involved and particularly so if you are unfairly treated. I have read and heard many references to people and incidents that I know from first hand experience are certainly not true, usually fourth or fifth hand and show the raconteur in a righteous and sometimes in their view a humorous role. When you have known some of those people you cannot imagine them being either original or humorous - unless unintentionally funny.

For years I have been fed up with reading about how Peter Swales came to be on the Board of Directors at Manchester City and recently I saw an article based on an interview with him in 1996. He said that he was in a pub and overheard two City directors talking about the group who had said they would take over City. He butted into their conversation and told Sidney Rose and John Humphreys that he was just the man to sort the problems for the club.

Rubbish.

Only this morning I checked my facts with Sidney and said to him, "I can't remember John ever going in a pub, unless it was for a meal after golf and the only pub you've been in to my knowledge is that one outside West Ham's ground that I took you into for a pint, when you and I came on the Underground from central London. To your amazement we stood shoulder to shoulder with both Hammers and City supporters alike, in a mutually friendly atmosphere that was a credit to all the fans. What a pity there is not more of that attitude these days. I know the facts, but you tell me them in your own words because I want to record the truth".

Sidney replied, "Around mid-1970 when City were one of the top teams, having won the Championship, The FA Cup and were about to win the European Cup Winners' Cup and the Football League Cup, several articles were published, rightly or wrongly it was later assumed by journalist friends of Swales, saying that a 'Mr. X' would like to put money into Manchester City. When the problems arose over Frank Johnson selling his shares to the consortium trying to take over City, the Board intended to bring a couple of Directors of our choice to counteract any imbalance. One of these was Robert (Reuben) Harris the Chairman of Great Universal Stores and the Directors asked the Secretary, Walter Griffiths, to try and find out who this 'Mr X' was and what it was all about. It turned out to be Peter Swales and John and myself were to invite him to the

Excelsior Hotel at Manchester Airport for lunch and to discuss the possibilites. After the meeting Swales asked for a few days to think about it and talk to his accountant and friend, Cedric Boardman. He came back to the Board and accepted the situation."

Thank you for the confirmation, Sidney.

Peter told me he had started his entrepreneurial career during his National Service by hiring coaches and selling the seats to other servicemen to go home on leave at weekends etc. Obviously a smart move and good luck to him. His well-charted career then centred around the growth industry of television in the mid 50s. He made a comparative fortune and worked very hard for it, but unfortunately and by his own later admission he thought the same principles could be applied to a top professional football club. His experience to date was with the non-league Altrincham; a mistake that is still prevalent and obvious in the game today.

Harris and Swales were duly brought on to the Board to balance the inevitable appointment of members from the Smith/Muir/Cussons consortium. Some slanted accounts make Swales out to be the great mediator in bringing the two sides to a reasonably civilised settlement. That, however, is far from the truth as I discovered years later that Swales had been running with the hares and hunting with the hounds. In other words, unknown to the existing Board he had been party to their discussions and strategies and then met with 'the opposition' and done deals for the future.

The credit for mediating and sorting out a reasonably acceptable settlement belongs to Frank Shepherd of the Manchester solicitors, Slater Heelis. Frank worked tirelessly and brilliantly to rescue a situation that would have devastated City. The fact that the existing Board members were retained together with their vast experience and football knowledge meant that the club was not left with just a Board of image-conscious takeover 'rookies'.

AFTER RELINQUISHING the reins at Maine Road and being very grateful for the quiet inquiries from other clubs, I spent more of my time with the junior teams and having been invited on to the Management Committee of the Lancashire Football League a year or so previously, was able to give more time to their affairs. Even as Chairman I used to watch the first half of many of our 'A' and

'B' team matches at the training ground we had rented at Cheadle, some seven miles from Maine Road, and then made a dash to do my official bits and pieces before the first team game. A few years later I was elected to the Council of the Lancashire Football Association as a Divisional Representative and faced life under the Presidency of the fearsome Bob Lord, which was an experience, as they say.

At the beginning of 1983 City were in trouble, not playing well and with a rather nondescript team. There was unrest within the club and the pressure was telling on Peter Swales. Our rather uneasy truce came under scrutiny and he wanted me out of the way in order to bring on some of his friends who he knew I would not work alongside. There was also talk of Cussons selling his shares to a Brewery and with the connivance of a bank man Swales told me a guarantee would be required from each Director to support further loans in addition to the already frightening financial situation. He knew full well there was no way I could come up with such an undertaking, particularly so if the money would be handled as it had been in recent times and it provided the ideal excuse to do what he had wanted for years to get me and the 'old school traditions' out of the way. He once admitted to me that it annoyed him to have the shadows of the past successes around him.

With hindsight – the greatest gift God never gave to man – there were several people I could have liased with in order to have stuck around and kept a weather eye open, but frankly I had put up with enough unpleasantness and I have always tried to stand by my convictions and not chop and change to suit my own purposes, something you frequently see, read and hear about, especially people in the public eye.

I wrote this letter on the 27th March 1983:

Dear Mr. Chairman,

With the impending share issue and the consequential financial requirements from the directors, at the present moment I am not in a position to assist the Club in this manner.

I am aware that seats on the Board are needed for those who will guarantee the finances of the Company, and in order to make my contribution to the future of Manchester City Football Club, I must ask you to accept my resignation from the Board of Directors in order to make a place available for such a situation.

As you appreciate, I have to take this decision with the utmost regret, but at the same time I am delighted to accept your kind offer of Honorary President of the Club for my lifetime, as detailed in our countersigned Company document.

My thanks and good wishes go to you and the other directors.

Yours etc.

Eric Alexander

Peter insisted that the title stipulated 'Honorary' as one paid director was coming and all Directors being paid was on the horizon and he made it very plain that he did not want me to receive one penny from City. He was soon to receive a huge salary of course, but as I have never had anything but an odd repayment for out of pocket expenses from the club, and it had cost my family a small fortune over the years, it did not overly concern me. I was very pleased to continue my association with Manchester City FC, which continues to this day.

When I learn of some of the sums paid to directors of football clubs today compared to what many of them have put into the game I shake my head in disbelief.

'Bureaucracy is a giant mechanism operated by Pygmies.'
Honore de Balzac

A SLIGHT diversion: my grandfather, father and in more recent years myself, have maintained that when City have a referee from Yorkshire we always seem to get the wrong end of the whistle. The exception for me was Keith Hackett, who had two magnificent games in the FA Cup Final of 1981 when Spurs beat Manchester City in the replay, and I can say that with complete honesty as a Director of the losing side. Incidentally, at the final whistle I leant across the aisle and offered my hand to one of the Spurs Directors and said, "Congratulations, well done, I think today you just about deserved to win it". He looked totally surprised and shook my hand, saying, "Do you really mean that?"

"Of course I do, somebody wins, somebody loses. It was a great game and that's what it's all about."

Hmm. That's what it used to be all about.

Mention of referees brings to mind two or three incidents concerning the venerable gentlemen in the middle, starting with the famous Roger Kirkpatrick who had City's game with West Bromwich Albion at Maine Road in the early seventies. During the course of the first half the Police Inspector in charge of operations that day asked the Secretary to bring me from the Box to the office, where he informed me that there had been a telephone warning that the IRA had planted a bomb inside the Maine Road ground and what did I think we should do about it.

I have to admit that my first thoughts were 'And up yours too, pal, you are the expert'. However, Mum would have been proud of me as breeding told in the end and we discussed the matter with the Secretary, coming to the conclusion that of the two alternatives, evacuating the ground and abandoning the game, or searching the stands and grounds and if nothing came to light, continuing the match, the searching was the better bet.

The Police made an announcement over the loudspeakers, Roger blew and stopped the game and the spectators were asked to search in the vicinity of their seats and standing positions for any sign of a suspicious box, parcel or similar. Mike Summerbee had the ball in his hands and immediately threw it to Roger, who caught it, shook it, put it to his ear and threw it back to Summerbee, who dropped it like a hot potato. The crowd roared and the situation was some what defused, if I can use that word. Everybody had a good look round for a few minutes whilst my fellow Directors discussed the matter. If nothing was evident I was all for continuing as I could foresee it becoming a regular ploy for some unscrupulous supporters to pull if their team was in trouble.

The Police and my 'colleagues' said as Chairman it was my final decision. 'Thank you very much,' I thought. Rather like throwing a drowning man both ends of the rope. I said we would carry on and once that decision had been made the Police said they thought it was the correct one. That didn't stop the other Directors, with the exception of John Humphreys and Sidney Rose, clearing off home at half-time. The poor old Albion Directors had to stick around as they were on the team coach which would not be leaving until after the game.

There have been subsequent incidents when supporters have invaded a pitch somewhere or other and attempted to sabotage a game, but thankfully it's never worked. I was extremely perturbed when I heard someone 'high up' in FIFA or UEFA say they want to abandon games if racist taunts or chants are heard and that they will support teams who walk off. This would lead to total chaos, it's very unfortunate but that's the way of the world and, regrettable though it is, I doubt that all the political correctness you could muster would satisfactorily cure it. Give your answer to those who mock and ridicule by your performance and ability, then it cannot be disputed.

On a lighter note I had a friend, the late Neil Midgley, who was a highly respected referee with a very good sense of humour, who could swear as well as any player if the occasion demanded. Neil also didn't brandish red or yellow cards at the drop of a hat or any apparent life-threatening tackle. "Get up, you bloody cissy" was the order of the day with many of the good old refs like him. I remember Johnny Hart telling me once playing against Wolves when somebody or other whacked City's outside left Roy Clarke and got away with it. Moments later City got a corner and Johnny got a dig in on Roy's behalf as the ball came into the penalty area, when he assumed the eyes of the players and the referee were fixed on the ball. Immediately he ran the length of the pitch to City's penalty area, to pull up and hear the ref's voice in his ear, "Another one of those, Harty, and it's you for the bath". It is doubtful that anybody else was aware of the rebuke and there were no histrionics. Incidentally, the referee was the highly respected one armed Alf Bond and Johnny has never forgotten the incident.

You know, looking back, it makes one wonder how the likes of Eddie Shimwell, Roy Hartle, Eric Westwood, Allenby Chilton, Norman Hunter, Tommy Smith and their colleagues with a strong but fair approach to the game would cope with today's attitudes. Somehow I cannot see any of those lads blowing kisses to the crowd when they scored.

Contrast that type of officiating with the final match of the 2006/07 season when City were at home to Middlesborough and the referee was Rob Styles, whom I've never met and may be a very nice man. However in my opinion, shared by a number of very experienced former players and managers, it was among the poorest displays of refereeing I could recall. I use the word 'display' because the impression came across that the referee was there to be the centre of attention, arms waving, pointing, standing over the ball and directing traffic at free-kicks instead of letting the team offended against get on with it. A crunching tackle in the first five minutes should have been a booking and would have calmed down what was an important European qualifying game for both teams. Shortly into the second half Ray Parlour, already booked, clobbered a City player with a fearsome tackle and just about everybody in the stadium expected a sending off, which would have left Boro with ten men. Style did nothing apart from utter a couple of words and award a free-kick.

Very obviously this gave the Middlesborough manager the opportunity to replace the player before he could transgress again - an unfair advantage. The match was a draw going into five minutes of injury time when Styles awarded City a penalty for a foul on a player. It would be unfair to comment on the validity of the decision when the ref's on the spot and I'm in the Directors Box yards away, but nobody seemed to have much dispute with the award, despite it being a critical point of the match. The goalkeeper saved the penalty, but within a minute there was a blatant handball in the Boro penalty area, which must have been seen by just about everybody in the ground bar the referee. We said afterwards that there should have been a further five minutes added time for the amount wasted by the referee's histrionics.

Where does this lead us? Well in Rob Styles' case less than a week later to centre spot in the FA Cup final, where he added to his chart topping card list and became the second referee to dismiss a finalist, a few minutes from the end.

Incidentally, nothing to do with refereeing but what a way to finish the football season, the FA Cup final settled by penalties. The most prestigious event of the English football year and the medals most cherished by players, apart from the fans who in my opinion deserve better.

Every absurdity has champions to defend it.

FRANCIS LEE and I have been friends since he went to City from Bolton Wanderers as a young and exciting player and I have admired his attitude, foresight, ambition and sheer hard work in providing for his future.

I suppose that these days if a player saves up a year's salary he will be more or less set up for life but not too long ago many finished up on the scrap heap or scraped a living when they ended their playing days. In a way it saddens you to think of the effort, dedication and loyalty put in by the great majority of yesterday's men, compared to the wranglings, moanings and outbursts by some of the well publicised star turns of today. I suppose that's life, but it does remind me of some of the men, and I emphasize 'men' in the true sense of the word, that I knew, employed or worked with and mutually respected.

Francis was a loyal 100 percenter as an employee and worked extremly hard to create a career to follow his footballing days. He was an industrious worker for his small business, was let down badly by his former friend and business partner whilst away on tour and during the next season trained and played during the day, spending the evenings and days off rebuilding his financial interests and by sheer hard work and dedication eventually created a multi-million pound operation.

The strain told and Francis was close to a breakdown when, near the end of the season, City sent him off on a fishing trip to Scotland, which worked wonders. All's well that ends well and Frannie is a very wealthy man who breeds racehorses, plays a mean game of golf and we exchange pleasantries when we meet up, generally these days at matches.

In 1993 Francis, encouraged by journalist Alec Johnson, decided to make a bid for Manchester City Football Club Limited, buying up shares and offering Peter Swales the opportunity to back out from the difficult and unpleasant position he had generated. Always messy, those sort of things create problems all over the place and whilst my views and opinion of Swales are obvious, I felt extremely concerned and sorry for his wife, Brenda, and their daughters who were as nice people as you could wish to meet.

Francis suffered threats from unknown sources when his stewardship of the Club failed badly during his few years in charge and to my mind that kind of thing is sad enough in politics and so on, but it is a really sick situation where so-called sport is concerned.

This period provided me with another angle to the inside of football and the buying out, or takeover syndrome. Older, perhaps wiser, and with many years in the game maybe I could reflect on past experiences and knowledge to offer advice and, if required, some assistance in the reshaping of the whole setup.

To his credit Francis will openly admit he tried to do things his way and it would probably have altered the course of later events and the future of the Club had he listened to, although not necessarily accepting, experienced advice.

I wrote the following letter to Francis as City Chairman:

21st September 1994

Dear Francis,

I appreciated our recent talk and I understand your ideas and objectives for the rebuilding of City. However, we did not have the time to go deeper into some areas where I see serious problems arising and, as in your words, I've been there and seen it all before, I believe I can make comment without giving the impression of trying to teach you how to suck eggs.

I know you have plans regarding them, but the outspokenly opposed and 'worthless' members of the old Board should have gone at the time of the completion of negotiations. The staff within the club, the public and the men themselves expected it. Their names still figure officially and prominently in the Club literature and to the outside world - especially the fans and the Press - nothing has changed, except for a new Chairman and some cosmetic treatment to the ground. The avowed intent and reason for supporting the 'takeover' regime was to see the happy family atmosphere for which City was famous and successful return to Maine Road and this can never, in my opinion, happen in current circumstances. As a typical example, I was given a very unpleasant time by one of them, still strutting around the club, for openly supporting and giving you glowing references in the Press during the opening shots of the campaign - now he's all over me.

Next to the team the the fans are the most important facet of any Club and our fans are not happy and starting to vote with their feet. I mix with a cross section and whilst I do not hold with mob rule, and without being intentionaly unkind or hypercritical, I do not think if Brian Horton won the next three FA Cups the fans would take to him. Nice man that he is, unfortunately he will always have the millstone round his neck that he was appointed by Swales and Maddocks. The Press virtually ignore him, eg. in controversial issues he is not among the managers quoted for an opinion. The fans want to read about their club and, frankly, we are being treated as an insignificant outfit, currently making up numbers - perhaps temporarily - in the Premiership. We are not being taken seriously and that really gets to the supporters.

We need an "Atkinson type" to fire up the press and the fans, somebody who will cause comment and concentrate attention on City. We have had publicity for all the wrong reasons during the past 20 years and need to repair the damage and get back up among the elite, both in fact and in the minds of the public. You can recall the rapport we had with the press and fans, and naturally within the Club during your halcyon days. The public are very fickle, as you are well aware, not too patient or tolerant and, when they stay away, very costly.

Incidentally, whilst not a great enthusiast for the man as a person, I suggested Ron before the appointment of Howard Kendall. He has always had exciting, attacking sides which are life blood to Maine Road crowds who have endured a generation of stodgy teams. He harbours a burning desire to prove United wrong in getting rid of him and I think he would jump at the chance to go for the throat. The fans would love it. You have been very sensible and I admire you for staying on the sidelines with a relatively low profile since the end of last season, but City need the Press on their side - Alec Johnson is a good mate of yours and he would be a first class "hands on" guide in this direction.

For my part, living over here makes it expensive and at times impractical to work on a day-to-day basis within the current club structure, but I am certain I have a part to play or contribute in the background, both from an experience and public relations point of view.

As you can imagine, I would relish the position of President, there having been only three others in the history of the Club, my grandfather, father and for a very short time Joe Smith.

Without being egotistical I enjoy quite a high profile in the football world and it would be a masterstroke to clear out the dead wood and appoint me as President. This would be well received by the hierarchy of football, who are watching events with barely concealed scepticism and would give a much needed credibility after the past years. The press and fans would see an obvious link with tradition and the good old days, and you would be seen to be carrying out some of the plans on which you based your campaign.

In my view you should act quickly, as by the end of September/early October the season could be finished as far as the fans are concerned and that would mean disaster all round. Fans have very short memories when times are not good and they, and the Press in particular will have their pound of flesh at the first signs of City not fulfilling the euphoric visions created at the end of last season. I doubt that there are many people around who have been involved on the inside of professional football as long as myself and I have seen most of it all before.

What I have said may not be very palatable or suit your requirements but it is an honest opinion, which you will always get from me - my only concern is not personal but, hopefully, in the interests of Manchester City Football Club.

I'll see you on Saturday, Mavis is coming with me for the first time in 12 years, so good luck.

My best wishes.

Yours sincerely
Eric

Alec Johnson wrote the following notes on 17 August 1995 and the content probably sounds better coming from him than me: (I don't know if they were ever published).

Former professional footballers could soon become tough, no-nonsense referees in English football. This revolutionary plan has already won the cautious backing of a section of current referees themselves, the Professional Footballers' Association and the clubs.

The plan to get ex-players in the middle with the whistle is the brainchild of Eric Alexander, the highly experienced former Chairman and Director of Manchester City. Alexander, as Vice President of the Lancashire Football Association, has already had talks with Gordon Taylor the Chief Executive of the PFA, and he is equally keen on the plan.

The Football League Referees and Linesmen Association has also given a guarded welcome to the proposals and further talks are to be held.

The idea is for current players to take their referees courses and eventually referee in Sunday League football, so that they would be ready to become top officials when their playing careers finished. One player reported to be enthusiastic and interested in joining up is Liverpool's Nigel Clough, son of former Nottingham Forest manager Brian Clough.

Alexander told me: "The Lancashire FA have set the ball rolling and Ray Cooper, our Vice Chairman of the Lancashire FA Referees Committee, has played a prominent role in the plan for professional players studying to become top referees".

Alexander feels it will strengthen the English game. "I have felt for some years that former players being put in charge of games will do nothing but good for the quality of our football. It is time to look at the whole system of the men in charge of the game, because at the moment it seems a case of refereeing by confrontation rather than with co-operation."

Francis Lee, the Manchester City Chairman and former City and England centre-forward, is just one of many former top players who believe the plan is a step in the right direction and he has also spoken to Taylor about the proposals. "We feel that putting former players in charge, once they have passed their examinations and become experienced can do nothing but good for the game, " says Alexander, "They know all the tricks the players can get up to because they have been in the game, and they will not be afraid to get tough right from the start. We believe the game will improve, let's see an end to swearing at officials and getting away with it as you can see so blatantly on television. But equally, let's have more commonsense when it comes to tough tackling in football, which is not a game for weaklings. There has always been a physical challenge involved and that is the way it should be and Joe Public wants to see soccer played as a mans game, so long as the challenges are fair. Taking away the referee's discretion, as has happened in recent years over the strong challenge, was a step in the wrong direction. The plans are at an early stage but we are all hoping that the former players getting out there in charge of the games will only be better for the standard of soccer the public are going to see as a result."

(This was written before we were invaded by foreign ballet dancers).

About the time of those comments, I made some notes regarding refereeing in general. No referee has ever been perfect, any more than a player or any other human being and referees can have bad or poor games in the same way as players, and this is accepted within the game. However, some refs have more poor games than others and the inconsistent ones should be weeded out for the good of the professional game where the stakes have become so high that a wrong or dubious decision can spell financial disaster or oblivion to a club, be they famous or local town. It is time for professional, full-time referees paid a good salary and if they are not up to it, then they go. To me the inconsistency of the application of the rules and the use of discretion is hugely apparent between the Premiership and the Football League and in recent times we have to suffer the input and regulations inspired by people from all over the World, many who appear to believe soccer is a non-contact pastime for wealthy show business theatricals, who expose their bodies, hug and kiss each other in typically manly fashion after scoring a goal and delay the restart by going all round the ground waving or shaking their fists at the crowd.

Professional refs could train with different clubs, get to know the players, lecture on the laws of the game, discuss incidents, use videos to illustrate points and generally live in the same atmosphere as the players and, hopefully, gain each other's respect. I have known numerous refs who have enjoyed the friendship and mutual feelings of the players for the game, but with the enormous financial pressures, real and theoretical, that are dominating the thinking of football officials worldwide, you have to feel some sympathy for the 'poor old ref', but as President Truman said, "If you can't take the heat, get out of the kitchen". The authorities appear to me to shoot themselves in the foot by indecisive and inconsistent comment and rulings presented to the public by unconvincing personell.

FOR YEARS I spoke out against a separate 'Premiership'-type league which we were assured would improve the English national team's chances and raise the standard of football throughout the game. I rest my case. I never believed that would be the case as the club's are clearly far too self-interested to give two hoots about the national team's fortunes. I was at a Rotary Charter night and I asked for questions after talking for a few minutes. The England team selection was called into debate, and whilst I was far from then England coach Sven-Göran Eriksson's biggest fan, I asked the audience to name all the English goalkeepers currently in the Premiership. At that time were just three regulars. They couldn't. So where is this great opportunity for English youth to blossom and mature?

Clubs are desparate to obtain finances by whatever means they can get away with and really the game is incidental to the God of money, especially with the credit crunch depriving several big operators in the field of sponsorship from spending money in the last year or so, or indeed seeing them go to the wall in a couple of cases. Football lacks the direction of people with grass roots in the game - people who used to put the interests of their own clubs high on the priority list, but took an overview on the game in general and its future. Nowadays so very, very few have football backgrounds, or a sense of tradition and competition. They are bankers, accountants, financiers, agents and self-made men who sometimes believe that once they have made money in one field, they can do it on the football field.

'*A self-made man who worships his creator.*'
John Bright

We used to laugh at the overseas games where the Germans invented diving, the Italians the cynical tackle and the South Americans the mortally-wounded player who two minutes after receiving the Last Rites raced fifty yards to fire home an unstoppable goal. Tragically this attitude pervades the British scene of today. Take Arsenal, originally the doyens of tradition both on and off the field (you used to have to produce your Birth Certificate, Passport and latest bank statement - even as the Chairman of the visiting club - to get into the Arsenal Boardroom). They have a foreign Manager, a team full of foreign players and a disciplinary record second to none. At the time of writing, some seventy red cards during nine seasons and a cynic could be excused for thinking 'win at any cost' had been their mantra. And yet Arsenal have been hugely successful and are a superb footballing team who do not need to resort to such tactics.

Some of the so-called top referees do not help much, encouraging confrontation rather than the essential co-operation. Referees used to be likened to small children in my youth, seen but not heard. You never remembered the name of a referee after a game, but these days when you see the refs name before a game you can be excused for thinking, 'Oh, God, not him again'.

TO THE last match at Maine Road against Southampton:

Having been asked for my memories it was pretty obvious that I would join thousands of others in quoting the famous City versus Spurs 'Ballet on Ice' in 1968, which saw us play some superb football on an icy, snowy surface to turn a deficit into a 4-1 victory, as my overriding receollection of the ground. However, there are other angles to memories, some amusing, some serious and occasionally sadness. For instance after the last derby against Manchester United at the old ground (and not because we won) I stayed in the Directors Box long after the ground had cleared and just looked around me, lost in a lifetime's nostalgia. I thought of my Grandfathers, Father and other members of both sides of the family, great players and managers, memorable games, delights and disappointments, pleasant thoughts of many friends and great characters like Joe Mercer and Matt Busby. I had no time, and I wonder why, for those who had caused nothing but trouble, conflict and unhappiness at what used to be known as 'the Happy Family club'. It was a moment for remembering the good times and to hell with the nothing people. Renowned for not showing emotion, I'm not ashamed to admit that I had a lump in my throat for quite some time.

One match to recall was in Spring 1947 when we played the last match of the season against Newport County at Maine Road. We had beaten Burnley, our nearest rivals, previously to ensure promotion back to the First Division with a goal scored by pre-war hero Alec Herd, father of David the Arsenal and Manchester United centre-forward who was born about 100 yards from Maine Road. Now we were the Champions and all five goals were scored by my boyhood hero, George Smith (I was always George in a kick about) and he was presented with the match ball. It was Roy Clarke's first game and when he played in the first match of the next season he created a record that still stands today, playing three consecutive games in the three divisions, Cardiff City in the Third, Manchester City in the Second and First.

Fans and officials remember their favourite positions (with regard to the stadium and football that is) and I have one which comes easily to mind, but will seem decidedly odd to some folk. Returning the following day from a match at Carlisle in September 1974 I was the victim of a road traffic accident and sustained a broken knee. Fortunately I stayed conscious and at the Carlisle Infirmary insisted on telephoning my friend and co-director at City, Sidney Rose the eminent surgeon, who arranged for temporary repair work and my free transfer to Manchester, where Norman Shaw, the club's consultant and a brilliant surgeon who mended many of our players, operated and gave me a great deal of confidence on the road to walking again.

I had stood down at the time as Chairman and Peter Swales would not allow the club's physios, Freddie Griffiths and Roy Bailey, to treat me at the ground, although the injuries had been sustained whilst on club business. I visited Freddie privately and spent part of each day for several weeks at first hobbling and finally running up and down the steps of the old Kippax Stand for hour after hour.

It was hellish to begin with, but it became a matter of pride to see how many times I could go from ground level to the top back of the stand and down again without a break. It worked and seven months later I played on the pitch for the City Staff versus the Manchester Media, making all the 'blood, sweat and tears' worthwhile. Tragically, Norman Shaw died soon afterwards at an early age and it was a great loss to both the medical profession as well as City and the many footballers who owed a great deal to his talents.

As I looked across Maine Road that Spring day my gaze wandered across to the gangways and steps of the Kippax and I felt a great sense of gratitude and affinity. It was a poignant and favourite memory for me.

An interesting reflection on that last match day was the fact that both my grandfathers, my mother and my father were at the opening of Maine Road Stadium, and on the closing day my wife, myself, our sons, daughters and their husbands and wives were present and two of my grandsons were City team mascots for the game, making it five generations in all.

I DID not realise why journalists had changed their style in recent years and I admit to having overlooked a vital fact. Time was that the local newspaper man scribbled furiously during the game in order to get the match report into the local "Pink" or "Green" Saturday evening edition with any notable incidents in the last 10 minutes or so going into the "Stop Press" margin. The lads from the Sundays had until about 7pm on the Saturday evening to do a slightly more considered view of the match and the others from the Monday's could reflect and pick out hopefully interesting items from the match or its aftermath. I could not understand why the Sundays and dailys talk about the problems different chairmen, managers and some disillusioned players appear to express at the weekends. I questioned an old and very experienced friend in "the trade", Richard Bott, and he came up with what satisfied me as a reasonable answer.

These days by 11.30pm on a Saturday evening most people who are interested have seen the goals and highlights of the main games on TV, the internet or their mobile phones, so the newspapermen have to find other aspects to satisfy their editors who have to sell the papers. He did not add that those viewers also had the somewhat dubious privilege of getting the pundits' usually bland opinions shoved down their throats unless like me you watch with the sound turned down. However, since his fall from grace, I miss Ron Atkinson and the mallaprops and spoonerisms for which he became famous. Some of these politically-correct experts should sit by the dugout if they want to further their education.

Sadly, many of my old sparring partners from the Press have retired to the Grand Word Factory in the Sky, but there are one or two of my old pals still around and it is a source of great pleasure to me and the cause of a few laughs when we meet at various matches. Years ago you mixed with the lads from the Press at home and away games and particularly on foreign trips. For example, I believe it was Derek Potter from the *Daily Express* and Peter Gardner *Manchester Evening News* who spent an afternoon with me travelling on the oldest paddle steamer in the World up the fjord to Lillehammer in Norway. It was a trip of several hours and I doubt we passed one word about football matters.

The football journalists trusted you and you trusted them to respect confidentiality when required. A reporter would only get one chance to let you down and he would be earmarked as a loser. His colleagues knew it, too. Only one man let me down and it was not critical, but he'd had it from then on as far as I was concerned and others knew and agreed with me.

Regularly you would be asked about some matter or other, Is it true? Anything in it? Any comment to make? You could truthfully say "Nothing in it" or "Yes" and elaborate but often it was "Look, there is something in it but it's at a tricky stage and I appreciate you're holding back at the moment. As soon as anything definite comes up, I'll let you know the details. Give me a ring later, or tomorrow or whenever."

It was fully appreciated that the lads had their professional job to do and to satisfy their Editor which is what it is all about. Many happy and interesting times were had, but I feel sure those still around will agree with me there was always mutual respect between myself and football journalists, many of whom seemed to understand the game better than some of their more recent bretheren. In fairness, the game has changed so much that not that many people understand it these days.

EXTRA TIME

A FOOTBALL club has to be run as a business. In this day and age more than any other everybody has to accept that fact, and that to some degree football is a branch of show business, certainly the entertainment industry. You have fans and you have performers, although some out of hours performances in recent times have received more publicity than on the pitch ones.

So many people come into football from totally unconnected businesses where they have made money, either by their own efforts, luck, inheritance or whatever and believe they can do the same with football. Professional football is a business and you are under the public microscope all the time. Everything you do is in the public eye, the bad with the good and that proves too much for some. They love the glory times, but when the chips come down, as inevitably they do even in the biggest of clubs, it is too much for some to handle and it is obvious they are not up to the job.

'Directors can tell you all the details, without knowing any of the facts.'

Earlier it has been mentioned that Directors were not paid in my time, so most were retired, self-employed or of independent means- which makes it pretty obvious that the available material was not always of great quality. But that was the way of the football world at that time. It needed new and younger blood on the League Management Committee and the Football Association. It is unfortunate, but I believe the changeovers would have been handled better and the game in safer and more sensible shape had the alterations and changeovers of the late-70s and the 80s come in gradually rather than the massive swing, with the Television moguls and paid Directors suddenly holding the balance of power. Financial brains are all very well, but very few - if any - had experience or feeling for football and in my view you cannot run a sport like you can for instance a supermarket, a television company, scrapmetal or a building company.

Sometimes I wish that I could be back in the thick of it, other times I think football is in a hole so let those who dug the hole climb out of it themselves. After all, who would want an outspoken traditionalist who can't stand egomania, ditherers and bullshit? I also have no millions to spare, but I do have the benefit of a lifetime at the sharp end. That doesn't seem to count for much these days, but I have to say it because when the final whistle is blown and I meet up with Little Albert he will no doubt give me a 'rollicking' (his words) if I have gone quietly and not said my piece.

Seriously, it would be interesting to be involved again, or at least a fly on the wall just to see how much is contributed by Directors and who knows anything about the game and can give the Manager a run for his money. I dare say that in many cases these days you would need to be a linguist or have the services of an interpreter. Even some with a sound knowledge of the English language seem to have convenient lapses at times.

TO MOST people the words 'professional football' imply the European scene, the Premier League and the Football League clubs (or whatever sponsor's name they may be under for the particular season). However, as the enthusiast will tell you, football goes a great deal deeper and further into the backwaters, and pockets in many cases, of thousands of relatively unsung heroes who keep our great game alive and well. I say 'heroes', but I had better correct that quickly and add heroines, as many ladies give up their time, efforts and finances to foster local football.

A good friend of mine, Ken Parker, Life Vice President and former Chairman of Morecambe, who won promotion from the Conference to the Football League in 2007 after years of trying, has told me many tales of non-League directors and officials digging deep into their own pockets to keep the game and local clubs functioning and players receiving their wages during difficult times. Wages may not be in the lunatic tens of thousands a week currently causing havoc with the finances of most big clubs, but in the Conference just as an example, wages can go from some £20,000 to £100,000 a year, which takes a bit of finding when you consider the gate receipts of most of those clubs. It's a good job there are generous locals and sponsoring companies enabling football to continue and develop at these levels and to provide for players who may have seen better days as well as the up and coming youngsters. Much as it may be a bit of a blow to a club's prospects of playing success, there are times when the transfer of a promising player can keep a club alive and well for another season or two and the officials of most of this type of club readily recognise this fact, although sometimes the average fan may growl a bit.

Directors and unpaid officials have to cover their own travelling expenses when attending away games, much in the same way as Football League directors had to do in my time. By heck, we must have been keen.

Mention of Ken and Morecambe reminds me that some dozen or more years ago Morecambe were in the Final of the Lancashire Cup, being played at Preston North End's ground which at that time had an artificial surface. I was a representative of the Lancashire Football Association and at half-time was talking to a former footballer and true gentleman for whom I have the greatest respect, Tom, now Sir Tom Finney. We were discussing the game and Tom asked what I thought of artificial playing surfaces. I commented on the changed pitch characteristics, different tackling techniques and so on, but joked it was all right if you had nothing else although it would never take the place of football. Tom gave a wry smile and said he didn't think I was far wrong. We soon slung them out of top class football and yet I understand the doyen of world football, Sepp Blatter, thinks all football should be played on artificial surfaces.

Bloody Hell. What next???!

IN RECENT times much has been said and written about 'tapping' or the making of illegal approaches to players and officials under contract to other clubs and companies, but this sort of thing, payments and 'incentives' has been going on in football since time immemorial. There were suspicions of 'professionalism' in football during the 1870s before legislation made payment to footballers legal and a great example is the 1906 scandal when Manchester City were found guilty of making illegal payments to players and the FA came down on the club in a manner that has never been repeated in the remotest fashion. Five Directors 'resigned' and 17 players were banned from playing again for City during their lifetimes. This number included most of City's FA Cup-winning side of 1904 and as there was a strong Manchester United influence on the Inquiry and some of the players then joined United, helping them to win the Cup in 1909, there was considerable resentment. Of course in those days players rarely moved to clubs at the other end of the country, or even county for that matter because of family, home and so on, which often dictated where a player could earn his living. The astronomic punishment eventually was repealed, but in a somewhat back-handed fashion as most of the players had finished their careers, although Billy Meredith proved to be a remarkable exception by coming back to City and playing Internationals for Wales and in City's first team until the ripe old age of 51. When you consider that these days somebody or other transgresses and gets fined what is usually a couple of weeks' 'salary' for the most blatant of offences and doesn't get banned from the game, it hardly bears comparison.

Certainly it makes you wonder what football and sport in general is coming to in this day and age and a couple of instances that probably today would be brushed aside as trivial concern Denis Law and Sir Bobby Robson. Denis was a skinny, bespectacled teenager with a squint but with a latent talent that could be seen by several discerning football people. Bill Shankly at Huddersfield Town took Denis, who started showing his ability which attracted some attention from scouts but nobody seemed willing to take a chance on the young lad, who by now had his wayward eyesight corrected. Dad knew Bill and both he and City Manager Les McDowall rated the chances of the emerging Law. Shankly regarded him highly and in later times admitted he had hoped to take him to Liverpool when he was the Manager at that club.

By now it was obvious to some that Denis really would make it and Les McDowall signed him in March 1960 for what at that time was a record £55,000, although transfer fees were never publically announced and generally it was guesswork on behalf of the Press or an insider getting a 'sweetener'. Law came into a City side that generally was past its best, with several great players on the verge of finishing, but he became outstanding and several managers were kicking themselves for their hesitation. One of these was Matt Busby at United and when Denis became a little disillusioned towards the end of the next season, approaches were made by the Italians who by now were attempting to entice top British players with huge, by comparison, salaries. The agent Gigi Peronace, who became friendly with Dad and myself and in later times arranged some matches for City, was the contact. Matt knew City would never sell Denis to United and Gigi told Dad years later that an 'arrangement' was made that should Law finish in Italy, United would be first in line for his transfer. As it happens Denis has said he always wanted to play for United, so when he had enough of the Italian scene, despite the attentions of other Italian clubs, he came back to Manchester. Contrary to the belief that people who run, or ran, football are 'thick' the scenario was obvious to those close to the action. Still, City received £115,000, although that only seems like one or two players weekly spends these days.

Before my Director days one of City's scouts told me that we had a young player, who eventually became an international defender, ready to sign, but went to another club and his father, who was a milkman, suddenly became the dairy owner.

That kind of thing never happened at our club. Even back in the days of my Grandfather and Father, City played it right by the book and the club lost out on many youngsters and established players by keeping well clear of inducements. To illustrate how you could lose young players before you could contract them I'll give you two examples of players who went on to make it big, but not at City. At the beginning of my involvement at the club, City had a pair of young forwards in the A team, Tony Brandwood and Steve Heighway, who looked as though they would make it into first team football at the highest level. They were great prospects. I don't know what happened to Tony and I can't recall him turning professional, but Steve, who was local and lived a stone's throw from the old Cheadle Rovers ground where we played our A and B team games, went to University and I'm told his tutor had something to do with the football team at Skelmersdale. Steve went from there to Liverpool, where he had an excellent and successful career, lasting 39 years all told, as since retiring as a player he coached the youth team at Anfield.

After my time there was a young lad that came through the youth set up called Ryan Wilson, who some thought might make a player. City's Chief Scout,

Ken Barnes, in particular, viewed him as a great prospect and told Ryan's dad Mr Wilson, himself a well-known former Rugby League player, that there would be a place for his son at City when he left school. They even shook hands on it. There were ways of getting round the offer of payments from elsewhere to tempt youngsters away by writing the equivalent amounts into the contract as future earnings, but City prevaricated over this and Brian Kidd, who had been on the staff at City and had returned to United, where he had begun his playing career and won, on his 19th birthday, the European Cup in 1968, scoring against Benfica in the final, persuaded Ryan to follow him over to Old Trafford. I think he was about 15 at this time, around 1989. Peter Swales certainly rued that one for the rest of his Chairmanship as Ryan Wilson changed his name to that of his mother's maiden name after his parents' divorce and Ryan Giggs became the best left winger in the country for nearly the next 20 years, winning more silverware than any other player in the British game's history. Unfortunately for Englishmen everywhere Ryan did not shed his father's nationality, becoming a Welsh, rather than English, international.

IN THE days when Sir Bobby Robson was plain Bobby Robson and the Manager of Ipswich Town and Lawrie McMenamy the Manager of Southampton, it seemed 'in the trade' that every time a club needed a manager Bobby or Lawrie was mentioned. Without being disrespectful this was generally due to their clubs not being considered top flight and their managers being willing to move up a notch or two. For some of us, however, both men stayed loyal to smaller clubs for years and whenever their names were in the frame, probably there were incentives to stay. Big fish in a little pool comes to mind. Usually there was a player in their teams who had a great career behind him and was a big influence in the dressing room. A sound move and good luck to them. Lawrie eventually moved to Sunderland and as some expected, more or less disappeared from view, whilst Bobby took on England and in my opinion was very unfortunate to lose the job, virtually to penalties in Italy. You can hardly blame the Manager when a player misses a penalty, can you? However Peter Swales was a big shot in the England set up by that time and I don't know if this had any bearing, but Swales and Robson had had their differences in the past. In one of his life stories Bobby relates that Swales once told him the England job did not warrant a full-time Manager. Probably it was in the early 80s that Peter told the City Board he had interviewed Robson about the City job (I can't recall who he would replace, we had so many managers around that time and by then Swales was running the club virtually single-handed), but said he would not suit us because if he didn't get his own way over anything he would take his ball home. I have not had much contact with Sir Bobby, but I have to say he always seemed to be having a moan about something or another. He kept Ipswich in the top flight, I thought he did well for England, had a very successful time on the Continent, a good spell with Newcastle and got over health problems, so he must have been a Manager of note.

On a lighter note, Bobby has come out with some classics in his time, my favourite being:

'The first ninety minutes are the most important.'

Talking of Sirs, I always think when the debate turns to those who have been overlooked for too long the name of Ronnie Moran, Liverpool's greatest servant, should be mentioned as typical of those who have missed out from 'the world that was'. Ronnie gave 50 years of service to Liverpool and football in general, as captain, trainer, assistant coach, caretaker-manager . . . the list goes on. With 31 (yes, thirty-one) major trophies or titles coming along the way, among them an incredible 13 league titles, he had some track record. And yet not even an MBE, or any other official recognition. In my RAF days MBE stood for 'My Bloody Efforts' OBE for 'Others Buggers' Efforts' and CBE for 'Clever Buggers' Efforts'. No further comment needed.

I MENTIONED earlier that it has been interesting to meet and be in the company of famous and well-known people and personalities over the years. Deliberately I separate famous from well-known as some have not been well known for the best of reasons, but generally enlightening to see and hear what makes some people tick.

I never really had what you could call sporting heroes as I grew up in a sports orientated atmosphere but it was quite exciting to see and watch some famous people at close quarters. For instance stars like Andy Williams, Matt Monroe,

Eddie Large (the original Manchester City fan), Dean Martin who I met at a 'do' in London, Jane Russell (of 'those' more in a minute) and politicians home and away. People like Ted Heath and Harold Wilson who, whatever their or your politics, are interesting to talk to about sport and in a sporting environment. The Dean Martin conversation took place when we were both at different functions in the same hotel, I have no idea what his was about, but mine was to do with the cosmetic industry, and during the pre-dinner drinks time both of us were a bit bored and struck up a conversation. As a matter of fact and rather a surprise to me he had a non-alcoholic drink and was interesting company during our few minutes chat. Ken Dodd, who I worked with on several National Coal Board projects, a quiet and interesting man away from the footlights and whose company I always enjoyed.

Jane Russell. There's a name to conjure with, I hear some of you older gentlemen sigh. Who would have thought from among my Manchester Grammar School classmates of nearly 60 years ago that it would be me who would actually meet and talk to the sex goddess of the mid and late-1940s. We had all read the outraged publicity and seen the preview pictures of Howard Hughes's controversial western 'The Outlaw', in which the very generously endowed Miss Russell struck a mild (by today's standards, but at that time a highly tittilating) and provocative pose in the haybarn and was the red hot topic of conversation among the male species of most generations. Obviously much older, but came up to expectations, kinky black boots and all.

One sportsman for whom I have had the highest regard is the golfer Arnold Palmer, who for me epitomises what professional sport is all about, sportsmen and women being paid to entertain the public who pay for that service and anticipated pleasure. You could be forgiven for getting the impression that some footballers think they are doing you a favour. Arnold has been a great communicator with the fans and set a very fine example, which in general has been followed by professional golfers, although all sports seem to be slipping a bit where manners and respect are concerned. I am grateful for the numerous occasions I have enjoyed his company and example and I have to admit that I was given his autograph on my sixtieth birthday.

Just as a quick aside, I spent some years designing bottle labels and packaging for the cosmetic industry and started a small perfumery unit on the Isle of Man,

Cynthia Lennon eventually becoming a business associate. I was doing some work with Ryder Cup star Dave Thomas on behalf of Seve Ballesteros when Dave got Arnold and Winnie Palmer interested in a special Men's Aftershave we were producing and for years afterwards I reckoned Arnold must have been the best smelling golfer on the circuit. No wonder he had crowds round him.

HAVING BEEN close to the game and its participants virtually all my life it should not surprise me that from the number of 'life' stories some managers and players have written for them, quite a few must have had more lives than Henry, our cat. The phrases 'wishful thinking', 'convenient and selective memory', 'vivid imagination' and 'fantasy world' sometimes come to mind when either reading or hearing of incidents, personalities and the game in general. Some get distorted by time or being handed on to others and often incidents and comments are claimed fourth or fifth-hand. I am sure we all appreciate that in speech making or after dinner talking, incidents and personalities are part and parcel of the business, but the way some claim authenticity or participation sometimes make you feel like bringing your dinner back up.

I like the man in question and for no other reason than I read this comment recently in his book, I witnessed the incident and have verified it with others present, I use this as an example of poetic licence. Rodney Marsh says he was so disappointed and disgusted after City lost the final of the Football League Cup at Wembley to Wolves in 1974 that he threw his Runners-Up medal into the crowd as he walked off the pitch, some time later regretted it, wrote to the Football Association pleading for a replacement, but was refused and asked if anybody still has his medal could he please have it back. Typical of Rodney's sense of humour.

At the end of the game he did indeed cause considerable embarrassment to both League and Club officials by slinking off to the dressing rooms on his own without joining his team-mates going up to the Royal Box to receive their Runners-Up mementos. Later he may have received a more satisfactory conclusion had he written to the Football League as it was their match and not the Football Association. Incidentally, Rod, it was a tankard and not a medal that the players received, so perhaps it was fortunate that you didn't chuck it into the crowd as you could have hurt someone.

Elsewhere it came as news to me that Swales wrote in a magazine sometime or another that City received 7,000 letters of protest at the time Rodney departed.

My memory is not too bad for an 'old fella' and that would seem to me approximately 6,982 more than the combined total we received when Joe Mercer and Malcolm Allison left Maine Road.

IN 2005, along with thousands of others and two well-known Manx figures renowned for their belief every week that United played brilliantly or were totally unlucky and the referee cost them the game, I sold my few remaining Manchester United shares to the family Glazer. Not that I had much choice in the matter.

The famous Welsh International Billy Meredith was given two of the original shares in United during his time at the club and later in life gave them to my father in token of friendship. Dad passed them on to me and I managed to obtain my 'rights' issues up until the time when shares reached ridiculous figures both from a price and issue point of view. When they reached their highest ever price, seeing the writing on the wall, I sold most of my shareholding and bought a brand new car for the first time in over 20 years. I resisted the temptation to get a red one.

Much has been said, screamed and written on this foreign takeover subject and it might be worthwhile quietly analysing the situation before joining in the anti-Glazer tirade. In the dim and distant past City, United and some clubs had initial share capital of 2,000 £1 shares and dividend was limited by FA regulations to 2.5%, it being only comparatively recently, say about 30 or so years ago, that share numbers and capital investment rocketed to the astronomical proportions of today. In most cases by the late 60s some 25% of the issued shares had been lost or for one reason or another become untraceable and some clubs made new, larger share issues. Generally this benefitted existing directors who had a large proportion of the available original shares and gave them a virtually unassailable grip on the clubs, providing of course they all sang from the same hymnsheet or were not tempted to sell out and feather their own nests. In my opinion many of the anti-Glazer brigade seem to overlook the fact that Martin Edwards and his United Director colleagues took the club on to the open market, making themselves multi, multi millionaires in the process. Now who is any man to criticize another for making himself a fortune? Very few get the chance and who are we to say what we would do given a similar opportunity. As Bill Shankly might have said, "They reared a monster".

So, once on the open market it could have been an American, a Russian, an oil Sheik, a Chinaman or the Man in the Moon that acquired those shares. It just so happens that Mr. Glazer was first on the scene and I've no idea how it will all work out and the rest of us will just have to wait and see. I joined Supporters United simply because as a Mancunian I did not want United to lose it's 'local' feel, although I fully appreciate that over the recent years the club has become a Worldwide marketing tool. Still, makes you wonder why the Directors didn't buy it for themselves?

Maybe Sepp Blatter is right (and I never thought I'd hear myself say that!) and the time has come for some sort of legislation, controlling and perhaps protecting the 'Britishness' of our National Game. There was talk recently of a cash injection into Liverpool by some Far Eastern country to take over from the Anfield club's American owners who had seemingly fallen out, well what would happen if there was a change of Government and the people decided they wanted their money back? Or suppose some prominent British clubs in all good faith accept funds from one source or another that later prove to be from the proceeds of illicit finance, such as drug dealing, illegal immigration or prostitution?

With the best politically-correct will available, all the foreign money, directors, managers and players have got to be a problem for the British game which could quickly lose both control and heritage. Three years ago when City played United for the last time at Maine Road, the City eleven consisted of two Danes, two Cameroonians, a Dutchman, an Irishman, an Australian, a Frenchman, a Bermudan, an Israeli and a Chinaman. One sub was a lad from London and from memory I think United had three Englishmen in their team. A far cry from the teams of Mike Doyle and Nobby Stiles who seemed to diet on raw meat for a week before Derby games. City won the Championship in 1968 with eleven Englishmen.

It makes you wonder what Old and Young Albert, Harold Hardman, Joe Mercer, Matt Busby and their contemporaries would make of it all?

One example I saw really hit home a few days after Liverpool's sensational winning of the European Cup in 2005. A lady journalist wrote a piece about British character and northern 'true grit' quoting the Liverpool success as a prime example of the aforementioned 'Northern Character'. Perhaps as a general overall writer and not a sporting one she overlooked the fact that of the 14 players representing Liverpool, Lancashire and the North, only two were English (admittedly both Scousers born and bred), the other twelve and the manager coming to our shores from other lands. However, the Union of European Football Associations would no doubt be delighted that it was truly a European team that triumphed.

Bill Shankly and I were friendly and used to pull each other's legs when we met up at games away from City or Liverpool. For instance I would ask him if the meat pies were as good as the famous ones at City and he would say he only went to watch City to get a pie at half time and after the game. No doubt Bill would have been thrilled to know of his beloved Liverpool's success, but he may have wondered what had happened to his highly organised youth policy and local talent.

Just one more observation on the current Consideration v Contempt, Friendships v Feuds and Respect v Rivalry and i will shut up about it. It is just that it stands out to me when opening a paper these days that you are confronted over your breakfast by the angry face of some manager or another getting millions a year and who could well afford a dose of sedatives before blasting off. Said manager would then obtain a little more repsect from the public at large. At such times I think of comparisons like Mourinho's glare with Dave Sexton's quiet grin, Arsène Wenger's stony look with Bertie Mee's beaming smile and Fergie's tonsils and bulging neck muscles with Matt Busby's fatherly demeanour. I know Matt could be hard as nails when required, but he kept that away from the public. End of sermon.

When Dad said all those years ago that he had seen the best of it all, I can understand now what he meant, although I don't suppose either of us could have foreseen British football falling into a foreign and avaricious abyss. OK, so I'm old fashioned by some people's standards and what we used to call in traditional jazz circles 'a mouldy fygge', but I believe that I know and understand my football as well as almost anybody in the game. I am disappointed with the general attitude and really feel sorry for the fans, the biased locals and the genuine enthusiasts alike. I expect added to that could be the diminishing opportunity for local or homegrown players to develop and make good in what is probably now the most lucrative profession available to mankind. The big thing was to play for your 'local' team, because it was your team. Ask the Doyles, Stiles, Finneys and

Lofthouses of this world. Now it seems that almost anybody will move anywhere for the money. I know that this seems silly coming from a staunch City man who has witnessed the multi-million pound takeover of the club by first a Thai Prime Minister and then Arabian oil billionaires and the signing of Robinho, Roque Santa Cruz and many others, but I can't help feeling that the soul is ebbing away from our game. It's understandable to a degree, I suppose, but the unhealthy and greed-ridden attitude which appears in some areas to overpower the 'old-fashioned concepts of sport and sportsmanship does stick in my craw.

I was prompted to dwell on this when I received my cheque from the Glazer takeover of Manchester United. I rushed off to the post Office to get it into my account before anyone changed their minds. 'All contributions gratefully received,' I thought. It will probably save me from flogging some of my City memorabilia to enable me to go on holiday this year. But joking aside I sincerely hope that this wave of foreign investors does not turn tidal, or indeed turtle. I knew nothing of the Glazers other than the articles which I read in the paper, and let's face it if you believe everything you read there then you really will believe anything! However one way or another I have experienced a takeover or two myself and there are many other angles to such matters than just putting up the money – even if it is borrowed and therefore not really yours in the first place.

MAYBE I should move with the times, but for the life of me I cannot see anything helpful to British football coming from foreign ownership of clubs, other than possible commercial advantages which are not generally in the interests of supporters. To me, the fans are still the whole point of professional football. I know all about the TV deals and sponsors pouring obscene amounts of money into the game in their own 'interests', which is understandable from their angle, but I have great difficulty in coming to terms with altering dates and times of kick-offs, club colours, changing historic crests, dealing with agents and so on . . .

What was it Oscar Wilde said?

'The old believe everything, the middle-aged suspect everything and the young know everything.'

Perhaps I'm not young enough to understand everything. Perhaps it is because I'm getting older or maybe being thick, but I find it difficult to understand the recent trend of investment into professional clubs by people who in the main have no background in football, or do not appear to realise that only a very small handful of clubs can be successful at any one time and nowadays, despite probably pleasing and exciting their fans over the season, are classed as failures if nothing has been won. If two or three British clubs form a 'Super League' or whatever only the top club will get the plaudits and the others will be deemed also-rans or failures, no doubt with the accompanying financial hazards. And let's face it, only a handful of European clubs could live in the Premiership. What is wrong with finishing in a respectable position in the current league systems if you have entertained and excited your paying supporters? At the present time fear seems to be the predominant factor and some clubs appear to have adapted their styles to the dreaded 'at no cost must we lose' attitude, which brings to my mind the Italian system of thirty and more years ago when they had a few effective but possibly the most boring teams in World football.

It was always accepted that there can only be one winner per competition. Equally hardly anybody remembered the runners-up. Now it is apparently unacceptable for a manager or club to go without a trophy. Where has the sporting attitude gone to have been replaced by this culture? It seems that even Sir Alex Ferguson or Arsene Wenger are not immune from criticism over their teams' performances - despite Fergie's men being League and World Champions as I write!

Malcolm Allison said nearly 40 years ago that there were few directors who genuinely understood the professional game, but many sought the perceived image of local celebrity status by being able to talk to and be seen with footballers. I've known directors from more clubs than one who would not go out on a Saturday evening if their team had lost or had a poor result. One of the pleasures in life and a privilege as an official was, and to some extent still is in my case, was being able to go back to the Golf Club or the local pub, just be one of the boys, and put the match and the football world to rights.

My friends and acquaintances have always respected the situation with my background, even before being directly involved, and we never discussed tricky matters which should be kept private or confidential. With strangers I play the mildly-interested and innocent football follower who only knows what he reads in the papers and gathers from the 'experts' on the box. Quite remarkable what one learns about life on the other side of the turnstiles and sometimes about oneself.

'The things some people want to know are usually none of their business.'

Fans and officials alike show and express their feelings, excitement and disappointment in different ways and I have never been one for leaping to my feet when my side score a goal or there is a controversial incident. It never ceases to amaze me that virtually all the occupants of Directors Boxes, countrywide officials and guests alike, jump up and shout when a goal is scored by their team. Dad and I used to sit side by side at the front of the Maine Road box, which was over the players' tunnel, so nobody could obstruct our view. Joe Mercer was a terrible twitcher and Dad reckoned he should wear shin pads when Joe sat next to him and Sir Alf Ramsey, when he was England Manager and very reserved with his comments, sitting next to me said in his rather manufactured tones, "I am always pleased to sit next to you, Mr Alexaaaander, because you don't talk and you don't twitch. Most people at clubs tell me how good certain players are and ask my thoughts on just about every ball that is played." Praise from the Master.

One of my pals, Brian Warburton, embarrasses me sometimes by telling people that I am the original 'Mr Cool', which, although I sit still is not really true as I do feel some emotions, particularly if somebody is unlucky and is blamed by many of the crowd, or a really good piece of football does not quite make it, there is a great finish or save by a defender or goalkeeper. Sometimes I'm afraid I tend to overlook what I believe is the advantage of having a lifetime in the game, playing it, discussing it with players, coaches and managers and I get a bit indignant and occasionally infuriated by some of the one-sided or patronising comments on radio, television or in the papers. I shouldn't really, because as we all ought to realise at the end of the day and despite the financial moguls, it is still a game and all about opinions. And may it ever be thus.

OPINIONS ON sport vary enormously and those within football are no exception. Some players and managers considered by the public and among various officials as worthy of note, or even idolised, can be held in very different estimation by those close to the action.

Prejudices affect fans. Newspaper articles are written to stimulate sales, comments stick and many a reputation has been spoiled and some given glowing admiration when within the game, and particularly in the dressing rooms, the recipient is well-known for 'hiding', cowardice, selfishness and worse. Behind the scenes there have been, and no doubt still are, players who the spectators imagine are great team men and who in reality have the distrust and scepticism of the other players. I'll give you an example. Years ago a player, revered by many fans and some reporters, was on the verge of leaving City for pastures new and I was approached by one of his team-mates, renowned for his dedication and loyalty to the club, who asked me if it was true the aforesaid player was on his way. I answered that as far as I knew, yes, and perhaps the way in which I replied prompted him to respond, 'About bloody time, the sooner the better. We're having a whip round in the dressing room to pay his fare'. Just goes to show, doesn't it?

Generally it is a forward that falls, literally, into that sort of category although several much lauded wingers have hidden when the going has got tough. When people were lost in admiration and extolling the superficial virtues of one World famous forward, Dad would say, "Fine in a good side when things are going well, but when things get tough doesn't cross the half-way line and never gets his knickers dirty." Many a true word spoken in jest.

Players can be quite different in the flesh to their perceived image on the pitch.

Television interviews sometimes highlight that point these days, but even nowadays it can still be deceptive and those who appear aggressive are often meek and mild off the pitch and those looking unable to say 'Boo, to a goose' can be quite outspoken and difficult. At such times I think of Jimmy Scoular, as tough, driving, aggressive and inspiring a captain as you could wish for and seen as such from the terraces, but when changed into a suit or whatever, smaller than you would have expected and with a quiet voice. Before the advent and take over by agents, it was quite surprising which players with whom it was easy to negotiate and those who took ages to mull over their futures, the most unlikely and quiet ones often proving the most difficult and frustrating with whom to agree terms.

Francis Lee was as tough a businessman as you come across in football, but sorting out a new deal for him usually took about twenty minutes, a cup of tea and handshakes all round.

Mention of contracts, times certainly change. Players used to be paid out of the gate and admission money and what was over covered the rest of the staff, transfers and so on. Season ticket sales and match admission money today, whilst astronomical by yesterday's standards just about pay a few players weekly salaries and don't forget that nowadays these are salaries and not weekly wages. I don't blame the players, good luck to them, but the system cannot be right when one of them commits a bad foul or misdemeanour he is fined a week's salary, which is peanuts to him.

Previously when a player was suspended, which was quite a sensation, he received no wages, bonuses and could not train or go near the ground. Probably the Human Rights people put the mockers on that one, but what do the fans who earn a working wage think? When you consider the money Pop stars get it makes you wonder, as professional football and show business are both audience-orientated, but if Pop stars have a couple of poor concerts or a bum record (sorry, disc or is it DVD?) it is soon reflected in their popularity and bookings. Footballers still get salaries even when playing badly, not breaking sweat, suspended or in dispute.

I don't want to harp on about this subject, but it stands out a mile even to the public at large that some of today's players do not realise they are born, to use an old expression. The boys of yesterday really had to work hard for their money which was, eventually, good by general standards but worlds apart from the millionaire type salaries of the modern day. Another thing, most players appreciated what was done for them and showed their gratitude by their response and general behaviour.

When I played, scouted, coached, directed or whatever, possession was the name of the game - if your team had the ball they were attacking - if they lost it they were defending and you retrieved it as soon as possible. If you gave the ball away you chased after it as if your life depended on it - your place in the team next week probably did. Now some of these wealthy stars stand still as though saying 'oooh, silly me' or roll around clutching some imaginary life threatening injury, which when the referee or nobody else takes any notice is miraculously cured in a couple of seconds. At times there are so many classy, deft touches when receiving the ball and often so long performing the clever stuff that opponents have moved back in numbers to cover by the time something progressive is attempted, leading, more often than not, to the ball being intercepted or passed to the opposition.

Showboating, which may lead to that lucrative Nike advert, is taking over from scoring goals and winning games.

On the lighter side, before advertising was recognised in the game and manufacturers took control, players were 'slipped a few bob' to paint up the stripes and logos on their boots when appearing in representative games or on TV. Did you ever notice when the trainer ran on the pitch to attend to a fallen warrior and the 'Sponge Bag' placed on the ground, the manufacturer's name or logo usually faced the cameras? Talking of sponge bags, did you hear about the famous and highly respected North Eastern centre-half, as tough as they come, who was hit by the ball at close range and in a very delicate spot? The trainer came on, put the cold sponge down the shorts to which the wounded player groaned, "Don't wash 'em, count 'em."

Perhaps some of my happiest memories in my lifetime at Manchester City came when Ken Barnes, Tony Book, Bobby Johnstone, Terry Farrell, Denis Law, Johnny Williamson and myself, sometimes along with visitors, met up in the Chief Scout's office at Maine Road and put the football world to rights. We would joke about FA coaching supremo Charlie Hughes and POMO, to our minds the mythical Position of Maximum Opportunity being taught to up and coming youngsters - where and where not to make an attempt on goal and other hilarious matters. Good job the likes of Rooney and Wright-Phillips were not around at that time to have their instinctive talent stifled or coached out of them. We consumed gallons of tea, had some wonderful reminiscences, very interesting discussions and plenty of laughter. Happy days.

Talking of happy days, before the City versus West Ham game in October 2005 I was grateful and pleased to be presented with the Football Association Medal in recognition of fifty years service to football. That medal is highly prized and does not come with coupons from the newspapers, so it was quite an unexpected honour and made me one up on Dad and Grandpa as it was the first one in Manchester City's history. The only snag appears to be that if anybody from the FA ever reads some of the comments in this book, they may want it back which will be another first in history.

> *'I wish my parents could have been present. My father would have liked what was said, and my mother would have believed it.'*
> Lyndon B. Johnson

PENALTIES

SOMETIMES I wonder where the future of football lies in our country, with the lack of opportunity to break into league teams and the seemingly endless importation of foreign players, lack of encouragement of competitive sport in the schools of today's world and the growing problem of obese children. I find it difficult to comprehend these namby-pambies who decree competitive sport at schools is bad for the children. What the blazes are they afraid of? Being sued? The white kids beating the black kids, the black kids beating the Asian kids, the girls beating the boys or what? No wonder we lag behind the world in so many ways with budding sports stars. And no wonder we have such a huge obesity timebomb being stored up amongst the younger generations.

When we were young and at school we played football with a tennis ball every lunch time, sometimes even in the rain, and swots who generally didn't have much of a clue joined in, admittedly on sufferance in some cases. Then as soon as you got home you played in the fields or headed and flicked a ball against a brick wall. I remember getting an old case ball - a real football - from my Dad about 1946 and we played until it was patched and worn beyond repair. You would be Peter Doherty or Jack Rowley or George Smith or maybe Stan Matthews, depending on who you supported, and the ball control of most kids was good even if they were not good players.

Even some of the top British footballers of today need a couple of touches to take a ball and move off. When I was growing up you had to take a ball in your stride to be any good and it gained you a yard on a player marking or attempting to tackle you. Among others, Bobby Charlton and Colin Bell were good at that and you only have to look at the Arsenal team of today and the way they control and pass a ball so smoothly to understand my point.

Obviously I appreciate that with the dreadful child abuse problem and the 'no ball games' in city housing estates kids chances are restricted in many ways, but there are wonderful facilities around. However, it seems to me that TV, gameboys, videos, computers and the likes of juvenile sex as taught in some junior schools - something we didn't get and had to find out for ourselves a lot later in our development - are spawning fat, unhealthy, burger-eating children whose eyesight is probably ruined by the time the are teenagers.

It also sickens me to see so many blatant cheats, particularly in the Premiership, more often than not getting away with conning the referee, who with the best will in the world cannot see everything that goes on. However that's what the assistant referees are supposed to be there to spot and you expect them to earn the considerable wages they receive in modern times. A Premiership referee receives annually £45,000 and over £500 per match, usually officiating about fifty games per season. Not bad, but when you realise that many of the players they 'control' are paid that much per week, it puts the whole sorry mess into perspective.

I cannot recall it ever taking place, but has anybody considered using four linesmen or assistant referees instead of two? In other words one linesman per quarter of the pitch. With all the affluence from advertising and television circulating in the administration of the game it could be worth a few extra wages to give it a try? FIFA have recently experimented with two referees, but I feel that taking it one stage further can only help get the majority of decisions right in an age when the pace of the game has increased to frighteningly electric proportions.

I was against it for a long time because it was always accepted that you usually got an even break over the season, but decisions and results are so critical now that I agree with those requesting a 'television eye' or whatever on the goal line. As television viewers we have all seen wrong decisions at some time or another and with the consequences being so vital to the very existence of some clubs and the financial problems of most of the others it must be obvious to all involved in football that this innovation has to be accepted as part of the professional game. Doubtless it will be costly and difficult to provide for some of the lesser professional clubs, but maybe some public-spirited players could donate a week's wages to help the sport that provides so generously for them and their futures.

Dream on, Alexander.

FIFA supremo Blatter appears dead against goalline technology. In this day and age just about every other sport has that kind of back up. Cricket, Tennis, both codes of Rugby. It is not flawless, but it has played a part in getting some key marginal decisions right, or as right as they can be given the evidence not available to the referee with the naked eye. So what is wrong with it that the football authorities deem it so bad? Television, or video recordings, are used sometimes to clarify incidents during the course of a match and have lead to revision of referees' decisions to award red cards, most notably the dismissal of Zinedine Zidane for that headbutt in the 2006 World Cup final. This is a sensible and welcome arrangement as the referee cannot see everything and there are some players around who should be awarded an Oscar rather than a free-kick. However, it does not seem quite fair to me that players can be repremanded or reprieved for individual crimes, whilst goals that should have been awarded and goals that were really not goals at all and should not have been awarded are irreversible. Surely that imbalance should be addressed.

It is pleasing to hear that referees and the football authorities are taking this situation to their discussion tables and when you consider that many other sports use filmed evidence for some decisions it makes sense. If acceptable it should cut out a fair amount of controversy, but then again what will some journalists and TV pundits find to fill up their spaces and phone-in shows?

IT WOULD be helpful to think of a plan to halt the way football is heading, with rising costs of admission, falling attendances, television's control and some people's attitude of live for today and to hell with tomorrow, but it will take a great deal of thought, cooperation and integrity to get some solidarity into the game. Cooperation is a word I have used with my tongue in my cheek as even thirty years or more ago when you attended a meeting of Chairmen at the Football League or Association, everybody who wanted to could have their say. For instance at the end of the meeting everybody would agree to cap transfers at, say,

£500,000, which was a daft figure even in those days. Then we all went home feeling pleased with ourselves, believing that football was safe from the knackers' yard for a while longer. Hardly. No sooner did some manager want a player than one of those same Chairmen would break all records to appease his manager, of whom he was usually in awe, and get his name in the papers.

So much for collective loyalty. In professional football there is no such animal.

What is it all coming to? We now have to implement FA instructions regarding youngsters, their possible vulnerability and the need for Criminal Record Bureau checks on all referees and officials involved with youngsters of both sexes. (Anybody who knows me, please note that is the first time the word 'sex' has appeared in this book.) It goes to show how much is involved in sorting out that sort of protection that in Lancashire alone some 1,200 referees have to be checked out each year, and overall under the auspices of the FA approximately 35,000 have to be checked. With the best will in the World that is an impossibility.

Directions are also concerned with things like the safety aspect of goalposts, goalnets, studs and so on, all of which really make sense when you consider the problems that can arise in today's society. Other instructions relate to religion and the care to be extended in avoiding fixtures on days affecting just about every religion. But I worry that if carried out to the letter how do we get to play at all without upsetting somebody, somewhere? In days of yore the game was played on Good Friday, Christmas Day and so on and it didn't seem to offend anybody. I know it took years to play professionally on a Sunday, but it eventually came to pass in 1973 and one or two well-known players did refuse to take part in such fixtures, but what would modern football be without two Sky games on a Sunday afternoon?

Today we all have to bow down to the god of television and play fixtures when we are instructed, no matter what inconvenience to supporters, whom I still keep saying are in my simple mind the reason for professional football. Recently City had to play Everton at quarter past eleven on a Sunday morning and some of the fans turned up wearing pyjamas and, judging by the standard of the game, a player or two was still half asleep.

It appears to ordinary people that the religion bit is getting somewhat out of hand, for instance I am aware that for many years there have been Maccabi and similar leagues solely for Jewish players in, for instance, both Manchester and London. Similar situations exist, among others Italian and South American leagues for people from those backgrounds. Seems fair enough to me, but at my time of life perhaps I'm a bit out of touch. After all, I was one of those who at the 'old' Wembley Stadium got a lump in my throat when we all sang 'Abide with Me' before the Cup Final. Still, I fail to see how there must be no religious or ethnical qualification in any league or club can be practical and to say the least would be a bit of a problem to monitor or administer. All this ethnical and international stuff made me wonder the other day if, on the 50th year anniversary of the Cold War between Soviet Russia and America, Presidents Joe Stalin and Harry Truman could have foreseen the confrontation being fought out on their behalf between Chelsea and Manchester United? President David Ben-Gurion, Israel's first Prime Minister, would probably have had a quiet smile, too.

'So many men, so many opinions'

Actually it would not be quite such a problem if some of them had opinions, rather than giving the paying public a blank look and seemingly allowing contentious issues to disappear under the Soho Square carpet (bedroom carpet in some cases?). In their defence it has to be recognised that representatives come from all walks of football life, schools, universities, minor leagues, and County associations as well as different levels of the professional game. It is obvious that some have far greater and wider reaching experience than others and in life there are always those with time and ambition, although I know from a lifetime among them that those qualifications do not always go hand in hand with ability and experience. Some ambitious ones can avoid being involved at times to protect their futures. It used to be said that 'FA' summed up what many of the representatives knew about the professional game and, judging by some more recent events and appointments, man-management in general. Having said that, there has to be a mix of professional and amateur backgrounds to protect the continuance and interest in playing the game. At the time of our visits to America and Australia nearly forty years ago it was pointed out that 'Soccer' more or less faded out as a pastime after the age of 18 or when leaving school because there was nowhere else to continue, as the professional or working future of the game didn't, or couldn't, attract the amount of interest necessary to really ensure people could create a livlihood around professional football. Hence the importance stressed to us, particularly in Australia, that visits from European teams played a very important part in the administration's efforts to popularise the game.

I like to believe that our British clubs can take some of the credit for both America and Australia now being major contenders on the World Association Football scene.

The Scots invented or discovered the Haggis. According to Oscar Wilde 'America was discovered several times before Columbus, but it was successfully hushed up'. The British discovered football, but sometimes you would not think so when you witness the lengths some foreign players and officials have gont to to produce a travesty of what the game was once all about. It makes you wonder what the big names of yesteryear, and even only a handful of years ago, would make of today's ill-tempered rivalry, open warfare and unsporting behaviour both on and off the field of play.

I must stress that in my opinion there have been many lads from outside Great Britain who have added to the attraction of our game and are fine examples of sportsmanship and ability for youngsters to admire and attempt to model themselves. Others are not, and sadly that kind of behaviour has seeped into homebred players over recent seasons.

HERE'S ONE that puzzles me . . . why do players have 'agents'?

I appreciate that some players are not as bright as others - like the defender who thought Paprika played for Arsenal - but surely they could use banks or solicitors for a reasonable fee. To hear of some agents, probably who know damn all about the game, getting a million or two for arranging a transfer that will probably only last a year or so is disgusting, particularly to the fan who gets an ordinary wage and in many cases pays an exhorbitant price for his match ticket, which in turn goes towards paying the agent and his player, leaving most clubs on the wrong side of the balance sheet. To read or hear of a 12 year-old with two agents is incredible and almost ranks with the tale going around that an almost 16 year-old is up for sale for some £15 million. Anybody with a background in the real game can tell you that there have been many 15 and 16 year-olds who have been potential worldbeaters, but by the time they reached 20 had either peaked and fallen away, just not made it or self-destructed. The exceptions who really made it through a full career are few and far between and you can probably name them without too much trouble. I thought the authorities were going to make rules and a register to control this developing side of the game, but I'll add that to the growing list of promises made and not kept by our lords and masters.

In these days of over-hyped and overpaid sportsmen – not just at football – perhaps it is worth recalling the deeds of probably the greatest sportsman ever to come from the British Isles, if not the World: Max Woosnam, who among other things captained Manchester City and England at football, won Wimbledon tennis titles, captained England in the Davis Cup, and won the gold medal at the 1920 Olympics in the Men's Doubles, hit a century at Lord's, played golf off a scratch handicap, scored a 147 break at snooker and once defeated Charlie Chaplin at table tennis by using a butter knife instead of a bat.

Not bad for an amateur who never received a penny for his sporting achievements.

Tragically Max broke his leg in the final match of the 1921/22 season against Newcastle United. Although he played again in 1923 he decided he could no longer reach the high standards he set himself and retired from football. He continued with other sports and had a successful business career, finishing up as a Director of ICI. He died in 1965 at the rather early age of 72.

Makes you wonder what he would have been worth in the current market.

IT IS difficult for me to see how some supposedly successful businessmen can be so sloppy when it comes to administering sport, but there again that kind of scenario has probably happened since professional sports commenced, although perhaps not with such serious consequences and we have to realise newspapers were the only media coverage in days of yore and it was usually low key. Today's multi-channel television, commercial radio (I nearly called it wireless), websites, newspapers and so on have to fill up their spaces to keep their advertisers happy and that sort of controversy is a gift from the Gods as a filler.

It is also interesting, although a bit frustrating, to read some of the comments about certain managers, coaches and so on and to be regaled by opinions of people who only know the face of things and not the opinions behind the scenes, or at the sharp end where contemporaries know the real facts and not just the popular conceptions. Very different and explains the silences or caustic comments when some popular name is bandied about in the papers, radio, television or in company. When you are aware of what some apparently suitable candidates for positions within the game are really like, you just shake your head and think about how much money they will be paid and how much more they will get on termination, when and if their possible short comings reach the light of day.

To bastardize Malvolio in Shakespeare's *Twelfth Night*:

'Some are born great, some achieve greatness and some have agents.'

Certainly there are some 'great survivors' around, a few of whom seem to have been with us for a lifetime. I know a of a small golf club who will be paying over £1,000 to a Sportsman's Dinner guest who will talk for about ten minutes and answer a few questions. He finished managing about thirty years ago and must be about 95 if he's a day.

Instead of football coming under one umbrella or authority, it is a pity that that there are several factions these days, which at times leads to confrontation and contention. We have the Football Association, the Football League and the Premiership in the professional world and some members being involved in more than one body, which with the best will in the World can lead to conflicting interests. Elsewhere I have mentioned the touching of forelocks to television and manufacturers and the changing of dates, times and so on, but where else would the FA find, for instance, the £27 million pounds it cost last year in expenditure on employees?

I don't suppose it is the fault of the FA, more likely to be from political correctness, but fancy replying when asked your job, "Goalpost Safety Administrator"?!

To give you an example of how wealth has affected those who have benefitted from it most, I can tell you a little story about a good friend of mine, a Manchester United season ticket holder, who was a big number in the retail world, with, among others, M&S and Littlewoods, had to retire early for medical reasons and has a disabled driver parking pass. He lives in Wilmslow, which has become a popular residential area for quite a number of the 'nouveau riche' footballing fraternity and recently told his friends about a demonstration of the attitude displayed by some of them and their families. He was about to reverse into the one remaining 'Disabled' space when a smart new car drove straight into the reserved spot. A young woman got out and my pal felt strongly enough about it to get out himself and point out to her that it was a disabled reserved space and he had been about to reverse into it. She turned away to do her shopping, saying over her shoulder, "So what, I'll just pay the fine." My friend Trevor was a bit put out by this and sought out a policewoman who said, "Oh, not her again, these footballer people think they own everything, park on double yellow lines and so on and pay the fines out of their loose change."

Very obviously not all of them fall into that category by any means, but to some the instant wealth suddenly thrust upon them takes some handling. Perhaps it is a pity that agents seem just to collect their monster fees and leave it at that, when some of their clients could do with a bit of guidance in the ways of the world.

I talked with some of my football colleagues about players, well-known within the game, who had been 'protected' by their clubs and escaped all sorts of problems when allegations were withdrawn, witnesses became 'uncertain' and possible prosecutions were dropped from sudden 'lack of evidence'. Doubtless frustrating for the authorities and it must have cost some clubs a fortune over the years. The artist in me thinks that there are some people in football who could be painted, but others might be better with a little whitewashing.

A PROBLEM that reared its ugly head about ten years ago, but has now settled down and become standard practice in the top professional game, is the Academy System. This was introduced in the Howard Wilkinson era and initially caused great antagonism in the junior set-ups of League clubs, who had their own well proven systems and leagues for many years.

Certainly the Lancashire Football League, representing all the Football League clubs in Lancashire, had a wonderful record over many decades going back to the 1930s and had been the breeding ground for many household names. District boundaries and so on were introduced, leading to some clubs searching for potential talent abroad and as distant as the Far East in some cases. I have a copy of the minutes of the last meeting of the LF League when all we Football League members of the Council had to retire following an instruction meeting and Bill Bancroft, the President of Blackburn Rovers, reported on the meeting and Mr Wilkinson's attitude.

Surprising that the minutes were not written on asbestos. However, things settled down and I am delighted that in many cases youngsters are coming through the system and it is providing the game with protection and instruction of high quality.

Howard Wilkinson travelled all round Europe looking at the set-ups that for years had left us behind and collected the best of the ideas in an attempt to set up our own 'skill factories'. Admirable sentiments, but unfortunately, despite being firmly on the right track, his attitude did not endear him to some people, which retarded progress and the cost-conscious directors of some clubs realised that by reducing the number of junior teams they could save money. How short-sighted can you get?

A reasonable transfer fee could fund an Academy, wages and equipment for years. However, overall rules and regulations have brought a level that was lacking and I believe all clubs have had some success, perhaps at differing levels, but success all the same. Youngsters of nine and upwards can go to professional clubs to work on skills, have the best of physio facilities and with child protection safeguards. The instructors, coaches and so on are chartered to high standards and the system can, in some cases, provide careers for those who perhaps were not great players themselves but can be motivators and communicators to a high level.

With my background and interest I am fortunate to be able to understand the situation and am grateful for the friendship and confidence of City's Academy staff, who have achieved considerable progress and have some half dozen former Academy lads currently in the first team squad, something to be proud of and I'm sure Jim Cassells and his team can take great satisfaction from what in these days of imported players is a significant achievement. There have always been dedicated people in the training of young potential footballers, people usually far from the spotlights, glamour and acclaim (and money) of the well publicised sides of football and people like Jim, whose own career was cut short by injury, spending his time trying to ensure youngsters have the opportunity to create a career in the game. Former City Captain Paul Power, possessor a high profile University degree, passes his expertise to up and coming talent rather than use his undoubted skills in the commercial or education areas of life.

I am all for the development of skills such as ball control, heading and so on, but I have great reservations about making kids of nine and ten play to 'systems'. They should be free spirits at that age and use their imagination and try and put into practice dribbling, shooting and the things they see on television, even if they cannot go to matches 'in the flesh'. Sometimes I suppose we overlook the fact that youngsters can watch all the best players in football by switching on the television and seeing their heroes doing the fancy bits, and unfortunately from time to time actions that disgrace the game. A few years ago, along with three of my colleagues from the Lancashire FA, I went to the Football Association Training Establishment at Lilleshall for a few days and found the experience rewarding and interesting. One thing that disturbed us, however, was the way youngsters were called back when at times they attempted to dribble past a defender. "Play it to one of your own team, back or sideways if necessary, but don't lose possession." Need I say more? A sausage machine comes to mind.

IN THE 1980s City played in the summer tournament on the Isle of Man and the manager and assistant manager, Billy McNeill and Jimmy Frizzell, were playing golf with me at the Castletown Links course where I have been a member for nearly sixty years. We were standing next to the 17th tee, renowned as one of the finest holes in Britain, waiting to drive off and it was about 4 o'clock in the afternoon, when I said to them, "If I have not gone across (from Man to England) to watch a game I will usually be found here at this time on a Saturday afternoon. It's about half-time and I'll wonder how City are getting on. Then I think to myself, 'So what. I can't change things theses days, so enjoy the golf.'"

Billy surveyed the wonderful scenery surrounding us on that great course and replied, "You're no' a bad judge, Eric!"

When I first drafted this book, several years ago, this was its end point. I had left the club I had been so in love with and so involved in for most of my life and that appeared to be an end to it. But life at City is never dull. I still go and watch most home games when I can and, as Honorary President, am always eager to bolster the youth production line which has been so fruitful a source of players over the years, albeit intermittently depending on the regime.

Kevin Keegan did a very good job at first, especially in returning City to the Premiership, but then shall we say 'ran out of steam'. He usually has an impressive start and everybody talks about him, but then he seems to me to have problems with people and perhaps wears his heart on his sleeve for all to see. When Kevin packed in I was delighted that Stuart Pearce took over as I had a high regard for him. He is a real one hundred percenter, but perhaps it was a little too early in his career to take the manager's position at a big club.

Of course the news of changes of ownership, and particularly manager, at City have become more and more frequent in the last 25 years. In 2007 former Thai Prime Minister Thaksin Shinawatra controversially took over the club, injecting millions of pounds into the transfer kitty for new boss Sven-Göran Eriksson to spend. Despite all that cash, I was delighted that Sven gave the likes of Micah Richards, Nedum Onuoha and Stephen Ireland their heads. Thaksin and Eriksson certainly changed the perception of City radically on the ever-growing landscape of football. However it did delight me when Mark Hughes was chosen as Eriksson's replacement in the summer of 2008 as I had been making my point about my belief in Hughes' abilities to various people at City for some time.

In fact I got on with Sven. Though the treatment he received prior to his dismissal was a bit harsh, it will be put down as just another chapter in City's turbulent history. The support that the fans showed him was fantastic during the 'Keep Sven' campaign, once it became known that Shinawatra was considering his future because of his 'failure' to reach the top four in the Premier League.

I was in the company of Sven at a Football Writers' Dinner in early 2008 and congratulated him on his progress to date with City. I told him how pleased many of us were that he was using the youngsters developed in our Academy, unlike many managers who prefer to turn the Premier League into a parade ground of foreign imports, many unknown, who come to gather fortunes, in many cases without any thought of loyalty. If their team does not have a good season then they will be off. Gone are the days when relegated clubs will be able to bounce back with a team full of players who are proving they are better than they were in the previous relegation season. Even only a few years ago when West Ham went down, players such as Michael Carrick and Marlon Harewood stayed with them. That simply won't happen in the future.

It is a real pleasure that my known choice of manager, Mark Hughes, is now in charge at City, although if Jules Verne were writing about City he would undoubtedly entitle it 'Around the World in 380 Days'. That's the way of the world these days and I hope the new regime respect tradition, history and human nature. I hear that their finances make the combined wealth of Abramovich and Shinawatra resemble a piggy bank. We will just have to wait and see what it brings to City. I hope they respect tradition, history and human nature and I wish Sheik Mansour and chairman Khaldoon Al Mubarak all the best in the world.

City have become the focus of the Press for various reasons. Mark Hughes keeps his opinions, feelings and temper quietly under control in the face of constant enquiries as to how long he might last in the job, so the TV and print journalists do not get much to get their teeth into. The problem is that means they are left to imagine situations, transfers and prices which cause laughter in the trade, but are taken as gospel by the public. Never believe anything about a signing until it actually happens, and then don;t believe what is revealed about the money involved, unless someone wants to make a point about breaking some record or other, or wants to kid another club on. The trouble is now that City will be mentioned every time a half-decent player comes up or wants a move, and often when they don't! They will be used by unscrupulous agents to bump up fees and be targets for clubs who want to generate a few extra million when selling their star players, whether City have the least interest in them or not. It's just possible transfer fees will rocket on the back of all this, and that could lead to clubs spending themselves into unheard of levels of debt, bringing them close to the brink of bankruptcy. The game has gone mad when over £100 million is being talked about as a transfer fee and what do potential team-mates make of all that when they play an equally critical part in a team's fortunes?

I do worry, too, where the opportunities lie for young British, and I emphasize 'British' as opposed to just English, players to gain experience and develop to International standards? Just imagine a few years ago Rangers and Celtic playing a full-blooded derby with just one Scotsman on the field, and that the referee?! What Gaelic or Anglo-Saxon phrase would be conjured up by a George Young or Billy McNeill faced with that situation?

OF COURSE the media is everything in the modern game. Players engender transfer moves through it, managers 'wage war' through it and former players earn their corn with their opinions. That's what it's all about. But the way the game has been covered has changed in so many ways. Commentators have become mere 'talkers over' the action, which has also crept into rugby and tennis, although golf's Peter Alliss remains the master of his art of understatement. Long may he continue.

I really can't abide monotonous delivery or, as in the case of John Motson the other highly excitable extreme "Oooooooh, did you see that?", "England are winning one none and if they'd scored then they would be leading two nil", "Both teams are trying to win" and so on. Why do we have people telling us what players should or should not do or have done, what the referee is thinking or what Sir Alex Ferguson will be saying to this or that player at half time.

Motty usually brings the words 'Manchester United' into play at some point even if he's ommentating on South Korea versus Afghanistan. Probably comes from being born in Salford. Mind you, being saddled with a nickname like 'Motty' can't make life any easier. I have known John since he started out and he is a decent chap, as is his contemporary Barry Davies, whose voice to me seems to tail off at the end of every sentence as though he's almost embarrassed by what he is saying, although he does a good job with the tennis at Wimbledon. Gary Lineker, a fine and highly respected player, has now become a blushing purveyor of the glaringly obvious and premeditated ad lib. Filling in the gap at half-time with expert, if in some cases somewhat inarticulate, opinions makes a good case for going to the kitchen to brew up or upstairs to spend a penny. I think Alan Hansen and Lee Dixon, Alan in particular, are worth listening to and are open in their criticism. I've no idea if the lads on the panels get paid enormous amounts by wayout dress designers, but at times it appears to me that some of them could be advertising for Oxfam or Age Concern.

Perhaps it is the mention of Age Concern that brings my wandering and ageing mind to Knighthoods in football, and if what we are forever reading in the papers about what young, and not so young, members of the profession get up to, it is to be hoped that they wear them.

'Practice safe eating, always use condiments.'

Over the years and among others we've had Sir Bobby Charlton (joked about in the game as still having his first wage packet unopened), Sir Geoff Hurst (you know, the West 'am lad who got a hat-trick in the World Cup Final and who seemed to disappear until Euro 2004 when he made some comments in one of the newspapers) and Sir Trevor Brookin' who took up commentatin'. But why not a Sir Norbert Stiles or a Sir Gordon Banks? Whilst the celebrated forwards, or frontmen, strikers or whatever they are called these days, were doing the business at one end Gordon and others very effectively were stopping the opponents scoring at the other. Sir Trevor was a good player, obviously because he won many caps for his country, but hardly excitin' and his somewhat bland and uncontroversial comments on TV make me wonder if he ever took over the England team they would have to play in grey instead of sponsor-dictated designer wear.

WHENEVER TALK turns to football in the press or in the pub endless debate necessarily ensues about who is the 'best'. Cristiano Ronaldo, through his agent, claims it is he. And who can doubt him after his wonderful displays in 2008, but 'best ever'? That's a whole other question. I will always believe it is impossible to compare goalkeeper with defender with midfield general with goalscorer. A keeper can make several great saves in a match, any one of which might be a goal, but the forward who nicks the winning goal at the death will always steal the headlines. It may be his only telling contribution, but I'll bet you he wins Man of the Match.

I saw recently a discussion on a certain satellite channel about the 'greatest goal ever'. It naturally focused purely on the Premier League era and on matches which that broadcaster had covered. Censored were all other goals. Does no-one remember the occasional goal scored by Billy Meredith, Duncan Edwards, Tom Finney, George Best, Stanley Mathews, Colin Bell, Bobby Charlton, Francis Lee, Peter Doherty, Brian Clough and Co? I have been led to believe that some of these lads, who get £100,000 a week or more these days, have to play a midweek game and then turn out on a Sunday too! Poor things must be a bit tired. They certainly spend long enough and expend enough of their energy telling us about how they are unable to give of their best.

Mind you, it's beginning to look as though managers are being selected, appointed and fired by fans and the Press, as much as by their immediate superiors. Certainly some managers who get mentioned for clubs and even national sides send a shudder down your spine when you know a bit more about them than the Man in the Street. We always looked into our managers' backgrounds. We didn't need a 'fit and proper persons' test to tell us what sort of human being we were seeking to employ. We found out ourselves by diligent investigation. That all seems to have gone by the by and consequently managerial tenures are becoming ever shorter.

It appears that the game has become the ultimate modern symbol of cold, hard cash. It's is now the Corporate Game, where it was Friendly, Family Football. The top professional football of today has become a vehicle of finance, image and advertising, which in my view is a pity because watching live football on a Saturday was a great release and relaxation after a hard working week. OK, so we have to move with the times and I am well aware of that in many fields, but it still saddens and disappoints me a wee bit. The poor old fan is copping rising prices yet again – to cope with all the salaries and so on – and I suppose it plays into the hands of the TV companies when it is cheaper to watch on the box than it is to attend games in person. But for me you will never take away the excitement of being at the game, caught up in the moment, the drama and the crowd. That is the magic of football. It's the football I would like back.

Can you imagine receiving (earning?) £50,000 or more a week, and what might you do with it? Two months and you could buy a house that would normally take 35 years of mortgage round your neck. I leave it for you to decide for yourself if anybody doing anything at all can be worth that kind of money. More to the point is the question - where does it all come from?

When the day of reckoning comes, and as sure as God made little apples it will do, how are the billions of pounds owed by all our major football clubs going to be paid back? All these funding machines which back them are classic 'never, never' operations. As one or two Building Societies and Banks in the last few years, even the largest and apparently most well set organisations can go belly up. It seems to me that when the whistle does blow on the day of reckoning, the financial turmoil of the 1920s and the parsimony of the 1930s will pale into insignificance.

WELL – AS 95% of television news reporters begin their pieces – I've put my world to rights, got a few things off my chest and maybe surprised one or two people, but as Carlyle said,

> *'Experience is the best of schoolmasters, although the school fees are heavy.'*

I've enjoyed remembering and writing some of this book, reminding myself of incidents, episodes and many friends made over the years. Some parts have been hard work and I don't envy 'real' authors who make their living from writing (I'd have starved after the first few pages).

Probably it is obvious that my main interest is what takes place 'on the pitch', but other aspects of football have been mentioned and I was involved in matters like obtaining many years of sponsorship for the Lancashire Senior Cup from the Isle of Man Tourist Board and my good friend, the late Peter Bagshawe who was Managing Director of Associated Tyre Specialists, ensured that Lancashire football benefitted from their long term funding of the ATS Trophy Competition. This type of support sometimes goes unnoticed or is perhaps taken for granted, but it is essential and the grass roots support and enthusiasm of people, often in the background, is critical to the survival and hopefully the progress of our great game. There is always room for more sponsors and financial assistance lower down from the 'glamour level'.

Thank you for your company and I hope that some, at least, of my disjointed tales and ramblings have interested you and that we are still friends. Please bear with me a few lines more whilst I bring the family up to date, then the whistle will blow and we all can change the subject,

One son, Angus, had a considerable talent and won the Island Golden Boot Award at one time, but his career was finished when an opponent broke his thigh. It was a very bad injury and the hospital thought it was the result of a road traffic accident when he arrived in Casualty. Two plates and seventeen screws were removed after two years and although his football was finished, he returned to golf and off a handicap around five he has played on many of the World's most famous courses and gets an invitation to watch the US Masters each years. Can't be bad. His sons, Elliott and George, are keen and could make it in the future and all of them are hot Go-Kart operators. My youngest grandson, Adam, at seven is too young to know how good he can be, but uses both feet so he's got a chance.

However, the star turn so far is my eldest grandaughter, Hannah, who as the only girl in the team was captain of her primary school team, got 'International' caps for the Isle of Man side in the Island Games, captained Nottingham Trent University Ladies team and guested for Nottingham Forest Ladies. I'm not sure how I would have explained that one to Cloughie. At five feet four inches she is as demure and feminine as they come and the last thing you expect would be that she has been a lady footballer. Her long-time boyfriend, soon to become husband, is not a footballer but a very nice man, all six feet seven of him, and a handy golfer. Without doubt the long and short of it. His only problem in our family is his support for Liverpool, but paling into insignificance when I have a son-in-law who actually enjoys telling people that he is a rabid Manchester United fan. I can't think of a printable comment, so on that note we'll sound the final whistle.

I hope to have a good few more years involvement and enjoyment out of this great game which, thankfully, transcends all borders, races, religions, colour of skin and prejudices.

FINAL WHISTLE

'THE ALEXANDERS have had almost as much influence on football and Manchester City as their glorious namesake had on the ancient Greeks'.

This description was once used by a newspaper and not by me, so please don't accuse me of boasting. It is, however, somewhat flattering as the piece was really about my mother, who, it declared, was the proudest admirer of this huge record of involvement and who was married to City as surely as to her husband, Albert. As previously mentioned, her father being a founder and shareholder, she watched the matches as a child; long before she met Dad, who she said had not been responsible for her initial football enthusiasm.

At the time of the unprecedented successes of the late Sixties she mentioned to me that she was glad that, at 77 years of age, Dad still went down to the ground most mornings. "It's his life," she declared. "At last he is being rewarded for the years spent travelling all over the place, far from the limelight, with the junior and budding players."

She said to me that it had been a long story, but a good one.

Sums it up, I reckon.